THE FOUR-LETTER WORD
THAT BUILDS CHARACTER

I enjoyed this book immensely. It has a nice combination of storytelling, current application of lessons learned, and bits of wisdom that tie it all together.

— Kim Eudy, Board member and Former President,
Lake Travis I.S.D.

An excellent tool for young adults, their parents and employers to teach work ethic and values that lead to a successful life. Richard's mixture of personal experiences and examples of noteworthy individuals will encourage you in the pursuit of your dreams.

— Tony Jeary, Mr. Presentation tm, Author of works including, *Life is a Series of Presentations*

Richard Battle's new book is a must read for those seeking to live a life of significance. In today's fast paced, winner take all society, it's truly refreshing to read a manuscript that focuses on the foundational values essential to achieving one's greatness. I would highly recommend this book to those wishing to become THEIR best.

— Byrd Baggett, Professional Speaker & Best-Selling Author

No businessperson, parent or co-worker should miss the opportunity to get energized by Richard Battle's book The Four Letter Word That Builds Character. *This book acts as a grappling hook to retrieve our rusty principles, tarnished morals, and forgotten lessons. Get a hot cup of coffee, read this book and start living a refreshed life.*

— James Bratton, President,
MST Constructors, Austin, Texas

The core concept of The Language of Conscience *is that we can judge ourselves, individually and as a society, by the values that we choose to pass on to our children. The quality of that transference of values both defines us and provides a foundation for their success in life. However, it is a difficult process in time and approach, and benefits from an outline and guide. Richard Battle has created an excellent example for such discussions that not only stimulates adult's thoughts and remembrances, but gives a basic checklist of key values for every parent or grandparent to follow in using their family experiences to properly ground the next generation.* The Four Letter Word That Builds Character *will help you conceptualize the family legacy of knowledge that you need to convey as well as material support. It is an excellent reference.*

— Tieman H. Dippel Jr., Author,
The New Legacy and *The Language of Conscience*

Richard has taken the basis of western civilization leadership as defined by the ancient Greeks and put it into an easy to read modern day analogy of what all would be leaders should strive to be and do. Leadership is character and the Greeks defined character, as "we are what we do." These are life lessons for all ages!

— Charles Cotten, Rotary International,
District 5730 Governor, 2004-2005

I thoroughly enjoyed reading this book. It is an interesting and insightful look into the core principles that has guided the development of our nation and society through many generations. It is an easy read of simple language and simple ideas that should be common knowledge to all of us. These fourteen principles are the bedrock that supports what we used to call common sense.

Success in life really is simpler than we think sometimes. The secret is to treat others as we wish to be treated and give a little more than is expected. This little book illustrates these simple truths in elegant parallels to a paper route that could have happened in any town in any state in America. Thanks for reminding me of the important things in business and life in general.

— David Hall, Training Supervisor,
Universal Computer Systems, Inc.

As the author of two books on acquiring skills to serve as an effective volunteer, I admire the way in which Richard Battle speaks to young adults on those important skills that they need to succeed…and he does it in a style that they will understand.

— Arthur Roberts, Senior Vice President,
Texas Association of Business and author of
Operating the Volunteer Organization and
Recognizing Your Role as a Volunteer

This book tells time and time again that it was our parents who instilled in us an ethos that guides us throughout life.

— Chick Simonds, J. Joseph & Associates Recruiters

Richard's philosophy of looking at the long view of your life instead of living for the moment lets a person make good decisions that will result in good outcomes. Living a life with his values will reduce your troubles and help you deal with the ones that come your way.

— Scott Sandahl, Author of *Water Ride* and *Power Trip*

The Four-Letter Word
that Builds Character

*For Clem & Pauline
Thanks for the many years of faithful friendship!
Richard Battle*

THE FOUR-LETTER WORD
THAT BUILDS CHARACTER

By

Richard V. Battle

Foreword by C. Lee Cooke

Afterword by William White

Copyright © 2005
Richard V. Battle
Austin, Texas

All Rights Reserved

Including those to reproduce this book or parts thereof
in any form for use by anyone other than
the original purchaser.

All Scripture quotations, unless otherwise noted, are taken from
The Holy Bible, New International Version (North American
Edition), copyright © 1973, 1978, 1984 by the International Bible
Society. Used by permission of Zondervan Publishing House

2005934228

ISBN 978-0-929174-02-0

Printed in the United States of America
at Morgan Printing in Austin, Texas

Also by Richard V. Battle

*The Volunteer Handbook —
How to Organize and Manage A Successful Organization*

Surviving Grief by God's Grace

Dedication

To my parents, Bill and Martha Battle, without whose unconditional love, support, and assistance I would not have learned the characteristics that have so enriched my life.

To Jerry Battle, my brother, whose love and support for his big brother has meant so much to my life.

Table of Contents

Acknowledgments

Foreword

Introduction 19

    1 – Be Responsible 23

    2 – You Will Achieve More with a Positive Attitude than a with Negative One 27

    3 – Have Confidence 35

    4 – The Value of Money 41

    5 – The Benefit of Deferred Gratification 47

    6 – Admit Your Mistakes and People Will Usually Forgive You 55

    7 – The Quality of Your Service Matters 63

    8 – Patience Must Be Learned 71

    9 – There is Synergy in Teamwork 77

    10 – The Best Leadership is by Example 83

    11 – Persist in the Face of Adversity 91

12 – A Job Well Done Will Be Rewarded	97
13 – The Essentialness of God's Good Will	103
14 – Your Threshold, Your Future, Your Choice	109
Afterword	117
Appendix A – Quotations	119
Appendix B – A-Z Characteristics of a Good Work Ethic	129
Appendix C – Battle's Bullets	131
Appendix D – Recommended Reading	133
Notes	135
Bibliography	137
Index	139

Acknowledgements

There are so many people who contributed to this work. It is difficult to thank all of them because of the years involved.

First, I appreciate the customers I served as a paperboy. In addition, I am grateful to the newspaper that gave me the opportunity to work and learn, and so greatly influenced me.

Secondly, encouragement is one of the greatest gifts we can give someone, and likewise receive. I truly appreciate the positive inspiration that I received from Logan Cummings, Kim Eudy, Tony Jeary, Byrd Baggett, Chick Simonds, Harvey Kronberg, Scott Sandahl, Lewis Timberlake, Nicole Kader, Scott Benson, Tieman H. "Skipper" Dippel, Jr., Charles Cotten, David Hall, Art Roberts, and James Bratton.

I especially appreciate the ideas and encouragement from Clarke Straughan. I hope I can return the favor someday.

Thanks to Carlan Cooper and C.B. Huchingson at KeyTrak for the confidence they placed in me.

Kelly Seiler did a terrific job editing my words. While husband, Rob, was serving in Iraq and daughter, Jordan, demanded her attention, she gave me invaluable assistance.

Thank you to Debbie Sheppard for her assistance designing the cover, and to Rick Henson for his photography.

Thank you to Lee Cooke, a long time friend and inspiration, for creating the time to write a foreword. I am grateful for his kind words and his contribution to this work.

I appreciate William (Bill) White, who led by example as CEO of Bell & Howell, for writing the afterword. I am grateful for the graciousness and friendship he offered me for many years and his positive words regarding this volume.

Thanks to my brother, Jerry, who assisted me during this job and has always been there for me.

Without the gifts and assistance of my parents, the experiences discussed within, and many others, would not have been possible. They have always been steadfast in their support of my efforts and my words are insufficient to communicate my gratitude.

This effort took time away from my daughter, Elizabeth. My hope is that she will benefit from the sacrifice in the future.

Finally, thanks to my wife, Laura, who encouraged me to proceed with this story, understood the diversion from our lives, and made innumerable suggestions that enhanced the finished work.

FOREWORD

This book reminds me of my time as a paperboy in the 1950's for the *Montgomery Advertiser* in my hometown of Marion, Alabama.

It encourages us to reflect on our values and how easy it is to let lessons learned earlier in life "slip a little."

Richard's book provides a refreshing re-acquaintance with bedrock values that enhance the chance for a better life, happier marriage, a stronger bond with family and for success in one's professional endeavors.

Each chapter inspires one to pause and reflect on what makes the reader the way he or she is today. The reader is given multiple examples, including those from historical figures, of each principle that is presented.

Mr. Battle's nuggets of life's values will increase the opportunity to guide as a parent, practice as a person with responsibility toward others, or can be adopted as a way to give life meaning and as a foundation of values for one's self.

Over the last fifty years, some professionals have been discredited or admonished due to the efforts of a few. It happened to the U.S. military during Vietnam and the recent Abu

Ghrab prison incident, top business leadership during Enron and WorldCom, Hollywood's top actors during McCarthyism, and political leadership during the Watergate scandals. Accountability and values of bygone eras were missing from the men and women who cast a stain on entire professions or groups of people. They lost touch with the basic guideposts that Richard Battle revisits again and again in this concise review of the principles of responsibility, hard work, and ethics brought forward by centuries of people interacting with people.

As we move into the twenty-first century with mistrust of leadership over the world in many walks of life, and as civilizations, from the West to the Middle East, to Asia, seek to find order and basic values in a world again at war with itself, this book provides a renewed and hopeful foundation.

Mr. Battle introduces the main beliefs of honesty, persistence, and courage to do the right thing and do it well, as they grew in him in that "first real job." This straightforward account of what a first job taught could and should be read by all. Choices are life's gift and how we make them and learn from them is Richard Battle's gift to the reader in, "*The Four Letter Word That Builds Character.*"

> C. Lee Cooke
> *Former Mayor of Austin, Texas*
> *Former President & CEO*
>   *of The Greater Austin Chamber of Commerce*
> *President & CEO, Habitek International*

Introduction

Click. It is the middle of the night. Thoughts rush into my head so rapidly that I can't sleep. I have to commit my ideas to paper out of a concern that I'll forget them by morning.

The question that creates my mental rush is simple enough. "What one thing did you learn from your first job?" This is my topic for a speaking exercise as part of a professional education program. We are to speak for only two minutes, but I can't stop thinking of the many lessons I'm compelled to address.

As I reflect on a career that has now spanned thirty years, I realize that I have never given much thought to the significant influence that my first job had on my life.

The unforeseen gift I unknowingly received at eleven years old has been invaluable. My first job taught me some of the greatest lessons of my life. My dad's company transferred him to Chicago. We moved from our, then small, Texas town outside of Dallas for a two-year period in the "Windy city."

As my horizons expanded, I recognized that I wanted more things than my generous allowance of fifty cents per week would afford me. A school friend of mine had an afternoon paper route with the, now-defunct, *Chicago American* newspaper. When I learned that he made $6 a week, he had my attention. For a pre-teenage boy in 1962, I couldn't believe it possible to earn that much money.

After substituting for my friend a few times, I knew that I would enjoy throwing papers to make money. Some months later, my friend gave up his paper route and the glorious position became all mine.

Sadly, most young people don't have the tremendous opportunity to learn the treasured lessons that I learned before I turned twelve. Unfortunately, there are probably laws against it.

Newspapers now employ adults to deliver our daily papers and they do it by driving down the middle of the street, barely getting the paper out of their car and into my driveway. When it rains, water runs down my drive and into the plastic bag that surrounds the paper. There is no personal contact with the carrier because I am billed and make my payment by mail. A solicitation is even included in my paper and a gift is expected at Christmas. If, for some reason, no paper is delivered, I have to call a central number to request one. Not surprisingly, this number is always busy and I end up having to go to the store to buy a paper.

Yes, I had many other jobs after my paper route ended and each one of them taught me important lessons. I mowed lawns, delivered prescriptions for a pharmacy, worked construction, installed meters for the city water department, umpired baseball games, and had an internship with a major department store. I even joke about how I shoveled sludge at a sewer plant one summer. The hot and humid weather contributed to making it the worst work I ever did. At the time, I felt fortunate because a very good friend of mine had to perform the task more frequently than I. Ultimately my friend went on to become an oral surgeon. I sometimes humorously wonder if I'd been directed to spend more time performing that job, would I, too, have been motivated to stay in school longer?

But, despite all the other jobs of my youth, the bedrock of my work ethic came from that paper route and the values my parents instilled in me. The values I adopted are not unique. No, they are timeless and proven and have benefited me when I lived by them. I believe **work is the four-letter word that builds character**. The fourteen principles in the chapters that follow are still a prescription for success in any endeavor. I am grateful to have received the instruction and example from my parents early and often in my life.

Unlike many children growing up before me, I didn't have to work to contribute to my family's income. We weren't rich, but we lived comfortably. I feel that those who didn't experience and learn from a job in their youth missed invaluable and irreplaceable life experiences and lessons. This book will share mine in the hope of communicating the lifelong impact of a first job.

Many jobs that young people hold can provide the same opportunities and lessons that I received. They will benefit by earning funds to attain the desires of their heart, develop self-confidence, and contribute to the quality of life for their family.

While this volume emphasizes the benefits and lessons derived from work, I strongly believe in the value of education. I would encourage people to take advantage of every educational opportunity available. However, some things cannot be learned in an educational environment alone.

In addition to the examples utilized from my first job, additional firsthand experiences that have corroborated the lessons I learned have been included. Illustrations and stories of other's experiences are also included.

There are three groups that I especially wish to benefit from this work. First and foremost, it is my greatest desire that young people entering the work force will learn lessons from the time tested truths within that will help them lead a successful and happy life. Secondly, I believe parents can use the characteristics included as an example to pass their own values to their children. Finally, I hope that employers can use these ideas as a valuable tool to lead, motivate and benefit their employees, their customers and their business.

We are blessed to live in a country where each individual has the liberty to pursue any career he or she desires. While every path has obstacles, success is possible. It is my fervent desire that the reader's dogged pursuit of the ideals that follow will lead to the fulfillment of his or her dreams.

Principle One

BE RESPONSIBLE

As I began my first job of throwing the afternoon *Chicago American* newspaper, I was ecstatic. I had taken another step toward growing up. I would earn my own money for the very first time and have fun doing it. Life felt good and came easy.

My new title, formerly called a paperboy, required working seven days a week. Monday through Saturday, I would receive the bundle of papers in the afternoon, fold them and put a rubber band around each one, put them into my bag with a shoulder sling, and load them onto my bicycle. I would then ride my route, covering a few miles, and deliver the papers to my customers, hoping to return home in time for supper.

On Sunday, I would rise long before dawn and repeat the process mentioned above, except I would finish before breakfast. It didn't take long to discover people's sensitivity, in the pre- 24-hour-television news era, about receiving their Sunday papers early in the morning.

Like the slogan of the U.S. Postal Service, my customers expected me to provide them their newspapers regardless of the weather or any personal hardships. It is amazing how all of us expect people to deliver quality service to us. It is also easy to forget the hard work and sacrifice they have to make in order to deliver their product.

Needless to say, the novelty of making "easy" money, by throwing newspapers, wore off quickly. Instead of looking forward to my daily regime, it surprisingly became work!

My parents used my first job as a great tool to teach me that the first characteristic of a good work ethic is to **BE RESPONSIBLE**. They stressed to me the importance of fulfilling my commitment to do the job that I agreed to do. My parents, rightfully, told me that it is easy to agree to do something, but much more difficult to follow through and do it. They added that I would develop a reputation for my actions and that this first job would set the stage for how people would view me in the future.

Being responsible also says that you will **GET THE JOB DONE**! Whatever it takes, however many hours it takes, regardless of the effort required, and with all of the help and support necessary, complete the job.

The difference between the successful person and others is often a very fine line. Anyone can do the easy job. A successful person will do the tough, but necessary things he and others don't want to do, that are required to be successful. The less successful person will rationalize why they didn't fulfill their responsibility and look to others to blame.

Another description that can be used to say someone is responsible is that they are **DEDICATED**. This means, according to one of my favorite quotes, "The ability and determination to complete a resolution long after the mood in which it was made is gone."

Being responsible also requires you to have the **DISCIPLINE** to remain focused on the job at hand when you would rather be doing something else. Sometimes when my friends asked me to play baseball, I had to refuse when I would have given anything to play. But, learning to be responsible and to fulfill my obligation early in life has paid dividends to me since that first job.

Abraham Lincoln serves as an excellent example. He had been elected president during the most trying of times in United States history. Division gripped the country and it descended into civil war shortly after his inauguration in March of 1861.

Slavery dominated the many domestic issues that disrupted the unity of the American people. Lincoln's ascension to office precipitated the secession of the southern states. Shortly thereafter, the war commenced. Lincoln suspended the writ of habeas corpus to control internal political threats. A financial crisis loomed. In 1862, his cabinet disagreed on many issues. His re-election in 1864 seemed improbable until the fortunes of war improved.

Through all of the challenges, Lincoln fulfilled his responsibilities. He endeavored in every action to preserve the Union and every decision displayed the impact of this goal. He relentlessly pursued a course of action despite internal and external opposition, and during difficult times in his personal life.

He accepted responsibility when mistakes occurred, and it revealed one of his finest qualities. His willingness to do so when others looked to repudiate responsibility revealed his character. Generals and cabinet members knew that he would not leave them to face failure alone and that he would give them credit for their successes.

Dictionary descriptions under "responsible" include: answerable, accountable, trustworthy, and dependable. Abraham Lincoln provided a fine example of executing his responsibilities as President. In fact, many feel he was the greatest President in United States history.

As a youth, I tried to be responsible and dedicated, which sometimes challenged me. Occasionally, I unhappily performed my job, but I did follow through on my commitment. The resulting lessons are worth more money than my college education and have positively affected me since that time.

Principle Two

YOU WILL ACHIEVE MORE WITH A POSITIVE ATTITUDE THAN WITH A NEGATIVE ONE

As I matured and worked on my new job, my dad would use the occasions where negative thoughts crept into my head to instruct me. Whenever I told him, "I can't do that," he would reply, "Can't never did anything!" He would concisely tell me that if I wanted to achieve anything, I had better change my attitude first. Secondly, I should not be afraid to attempt things that were discovered outside my comfort zone. While I haven't always succeeded, I have accomplished more because of the value of this lesson he instilled into me.

Many times on my paper route, I thought I couldn't do something and it made me apprehensive. If I had to wait on the papers to arrive, which meant I would be late delivering to my customers, it would upset me. When bad weather occurred,

I had to ignore it and proceed to fulfill my responsibility. People rejecting my efforts to sell them a subscription to the paper hurt my feelings, but I had to learn to disregard my feelings because the rejection had not been personal. It made me very uncomfortable to have to repeatedly ask people to pay their weekly subscription, but I had to persist to meet my work requirements. Automotive giant Henry Ford said, "Whether you think you can, or think you can't, you're right." When we believe that we can't do something, we have doomed ourselves to failure, or worse, the abandonment of attempting anything with risk.

Children are more inclined to attempt something than adults because they have not experienced failure and the accompanying negative feedback from people. There is a quote that describes children perfectly which says, "It is amazing what one can accomplish when one doesn't know what one can't do." My six-year-old daughter, Elizabeth, never ceases to amaze me. She is willing to try anything without considering failure or its consequence. Elizabeth has learned to swim, ride horses, and participate in gymnastics without any doubt of success.

As we go through life, we need to maintain this approach in life. An often-overlooked benefit in goal setting is that, even when a goal is not fully achieved, a person achieves more than if they never set the goal. An illustration of this is found in an old Native American expression that says, "It is better to aim at the sky and strike an eagle, than to aim at an eagle and strike a rock."

There are two expressions that illustrate my life-tested beliefs about the experiences we face that challenge us. The first expression is, "**THINGS COULD ALWAYS BE WORSE.**" In most of the experiences of life, we can find someone who is worse off than we are and something that could be worse about what we are experiencing. In "*Surviving Grief By God's Grace,*" I wrote about this lesson concerning the loss of our son, John. People ask me, "How could it have been worse?" As I explain to them, I could have never experienced the joy of my son at all. He could have lived an even shorter life than he did. I could have lost my wife, Laura, at the same time, and John could have suffered from an illness before he passed away. Losing my son has been the worst experience of my life, yet I learned that as long as you have hope, things can always be worse.

The second is, "**THINGS ARE NEVER AS BAD AS THEY APPEAR AT THE MOMENT.**" It is easy to get caught up in the present and believe that an event is catastrophic. One advantage of maturing is that we have more life experiences to draw from when we encounter something that threatens us. More often than not, the current crisis isn't as life changing over the course of time as it is "in the moment."

A work associate expressed it another way. He said, "Three years from now, you won't even remember what seems so traumatic to you now. Can you remember what troubled you three years ago?" His reasoning is accurate and beneficial.

One Saturday, two months after our son passed away, we had friends coming by for an evening social visit. During the afternoon, as we prepared for their arrival, our water softener broke, we found a leak in our guest bathroom and our water heater blew up. To top it all off, when we opened the door to the water heater, we discovered termites. Earlier, I would have totally lost my composure, but our recent experience had put these minor inconveniences into their proper perspective. Other examples could be, losing a job, losing money on an investment, losing a girlfriend or boyfriend, losing a sales contest, or losing a sports game. It is during these times that we need to remember the long-term perspective to help us weather the stress on our attitude in the short term.

My life experiences since childhood have confirmed a phenomenon that my parent's training instilled in me. In simple terms, I believe that the outlook people have in life generally falls into one of two categories.

The first group always sees things negatively. They observe things as obstacles, problems, difficulties, or bad luck; it's always someone else's fault or they come up with other reasons that make them feel the deck of cards in life is stacked against them. This kind of attitude affects not only their daily life, but also their life as a whole.

Most of us have experienced people like this. Not only does their negativity adversely influence their life, but if allowed, it will impact other's lives in undesirable ways as well. These are the people who will always tell you why you shouldn't seek your dreams because failure is probable. These people will also be quick to remind you with, "I told you so," if you fail in an effort. Instead of assisting you in your effort, once you have determined to undertake it, they will stand aside, waiting to make themselves feel better if you fail.

If you allow it, daily conversation with some of these people can be enough to sour your attitude. I worked for several years with a gentleman who, every time I called him and asked, "How are you doing?" he always replied, "Not worth a d_mn." Instead of allowing his pessimism to affect me, I purposely tried each time I called to give him a reason to feel better. While I don't know if I succeeded in helping him, it did prevent me from succumbing to his philosophy.

Life has a way of attempting to steer people into adopting a pessimistic viewpoint. It is much easier to adopt this philosophy because you can then minimize effort, risk, heartache, loss, discomfort, and failure. Once they find their comfort zone, they settle into a life of narrow boundaries where they seldom change and are infrequently surprised by what happens.

The second group's attitude is the one that I am thankful to have learned and/or inherited, which views life positively. This smaller group views problems as opportunities. They use every experience as an event to be learned from in order to improve their future. The bitterness of a setback gives them the perspective with which to appreciate and savor every success. They are willing to take risks in life because they understand that is the only way they are ever going to change their circumstances.

In addition to achieving more in life, I am convinced this group is also happier. If you observe carefully, you will find that the people who are genuinely happy most of the time have a positive outlook on life. They are friendlier to everyone. They are willing to assist you in your attempt to attain your dreams, even if you achieve more than they have. They are thrilled when you succeed and enjoy celebrating your successes. More importantly, they are there to pick you up when you suffer a setback and will encourage you to not give up, but to try, try, try again.

A positive outlook on life provides the confidence to maximize the opportunities that present themselves to you and the inner strength to face life's difficulties. Once we have a positive attitude, we have to beware of another enemy, which is overconfidence or arrogance. If we become too positive, we can lose touch with reality, which will cause us to misjudge people and situations. As an old expression says, "We may become too big for our britches." This is especially dangerous when we are on top of the world with no end in sight to our achievements. Life isn't always easy and there will be setbacks in life, in addition to successes.

For most of his life, few would have predicted that Ronald Reagan would ever be elected President of the United States. A radio broadcaster and actor, he won his first election for Governor of California in his fifties.

As an elected official, Reagan had those who agreed and disagreed with his political views. Still, many people beloved him because of his positive attitude and approach toward life. He related to every man, and almost every man related to him.

"His real heroes were common folk who performed uncommon feats of self-denial and courage."[1] These qualities were highlighted in the abundant remembrances offered at his death.

As President, Reagan had a vision of where to lead the country, the principles to stay focused to achieve his objectives, and the positive outlook to persevere in spite of opposition and reversals. After a tumultuous period, he restored dignity to the Presidency.

Instituting policies that eventually ended the Cold War stand as one of his greatest legacies. President Reagan pursued bold initiatives with conviction while some doubted his competence.

His willingness to walk away from negotiations with the Soviets at their summit meeting in Reykjavik, Iceland in 1986 demonstrated his style of negotiating from confidence and strength rather than fear. The resulting paradigm shift, when combined with other strategies, culminated with the Berlin Wall falling in 1989 and the collapse of the Soviet Union in 1991. Victory in the Cold War resulted without firing a shot, and President Reagan made a significant contribution to the victory.

Known as "The Great Communicator," few could equal Reagan's use of humor. His jokes entertained people and helped them to better understand his message. He often poked fun at himself, which helped people relate to him.

Reagan exuded self-assurance, and more importantly, he displayed confidence in the ability of others. His optimism inspired people to be more than they were, and his example demonstrated the possibility to achieve one's dreams. The resulting pride in America and being an American resulted in a period of peace and prosperity. President Reagan's positive attitude and leadership contributed as much as any policy to the positive impact produced by his presidency.

In summary, people who view life negatively will see situations as problems and, thus, miss opportunities. Adversity will oppress them and they will miss the lessons and confidence to be learned from enduring until it abates.

People who are overconfident display a positive attitude through good times and bad, to the point that they are not credible. They are so confident in themselves that they put people off and miss out on many of the blessings of life.

People who view life positively see situations as opportunities and look for ways to benefit from them. They face adversity with the perspective that it will usually be a relatively short-term situation and that lessons can be gained to benefit them for the remainder of their life.

We all have a choice to make regarding the way we view life. Our choices will determine how we view everything.

Principle Three

HAVE CONFIDENCE

Throwing the paper daily never created fear or doubt in me, but two other job obligations did. Collecting subscription fees and soliciting new customers had not been part of my job when I substituted for my friend. But, they became a requirement immediately when I assumed the job full-time. While these responsibilities created obstacles for me at the time, I later recognized them as gifts. They gave me my first opportunity and responsibility for asking people to pay for a value received and handling that money. All of my experiences closing the deal have been influenced by what I learned then.

At that time, *The Chicago American* newspaper cost seventy cents per week for seven-day- a-week home delivery. It seemed like so much money then, and so little now, after years and inflation have affected our economy. Today, newspapers generally mail an invoice to their subscribers who remit their payment by check or credit card. Carriers are never involved in the financial transaction between the paper and the customer. Unlike today, my responsibility included collecting the seventy cents fee per week from each of my customers. Beginning on Thursday, I would deliver the paper and ask for the week's subscription fee. If fortune smiled on me, most people would pay immediately and I would have minimal collection issues. On the other hand, some customers required several requests before I received payment. It is difficult enough for a young person to ask an adult for money, standing on the adult's doorstep, but it is even more difficult to repeatedly ask someone who has not met his or her financial commitment. Yet, another valuable lesson was ingrained in me from the experience.

I carried extra cash, and made change for people because I couldn't accept any other form of payment. I distinctly remember arriving home one day and discovering to my horror, that I had lost some of the money that I believed I had securely tucked into my pocket. The government didn't come to bail me out, and thankfully, my parents allowed me to suffer the loss. Instead, I made less money that week and from that point on, I received and transported my money very carefully.

In addition, I had the challenge of soliciting new customers to expand my small business and replacing customers who cancelled their subscriptions for one reason or another. Again, this meant going door-to-door, in hopes of acquiring new customers. Attempting to persuade an adult on their front doorstep why they should commit to spending their money for the newspaper, and relying on me to deliver it to them each day on a timely basis, proved a challenge. Today's carriers have no concept of this, as newspapers use telephone solicitation, mail-outs, store displays and other techniques to acquire new subscribers. While I did not relish this task, nor did I do it every day, I realized quickly that my success directly depended on gaining and retaining subscribers. This realization changed my attitude from one of "completing a chore" to one of "taking advantage of an opportunity to improve my results."

Both of the tasks I detailed above provided me with invaluable experience in dealing with people and handling money. They instilled into me the confidence to ask someone for payment for a service rendered. Approaching a stranger to ask for a new subscription proved more difficult than asking an existing customer for payment. This experience eliminated my fear of what the sales profession calls "cold calling." If I could go to the home of a stranger and ask for his business, how much easier would it be to go to his office and ask for the same? Significantly, I discovered.

I also benefited by learning how to better communicate with older, better educated, and more mature people than I was. I learned to communicate concisely the benefits of a business proposition because I never knew, standing on that front porch, when my prospective subscriber would end my presentation with the dreaded "NO" response. Secondly, the experience of asking people to buy a service from me instilled into me a belief in my ability, and the boldness to ask others to also subscribe. Finally, my earliest experience with rejection has helped me to face it in my career. Unless you are especially blessed or sheltered, you, too, will face it. **The earlier you face** rejection, and learn how to respond to it, the better you will be prepared for it when it comes in the future.

When you are very young, you are fearless. Young children will attempt things that strike fear into adults without hesitation. But, by the time you reach ten or eleven, you have encountered enough of life to know that not every experience always goes your way. You have experienced anxiety and the doubts it creates. By the time I acquired my paper route, I had been exposed to life enough to recognize fear, but not the conviction to know how to respond to it.

It would have been much easier to quit my paper route because I found one of its elements too difficult. Thankfully, I persisted and stepped into an unknown area and risked failure, but more importantly, aimed for success. The tasks that seemed difficult, then, gave me a foundation of confidence, which I have benefited from in every area of my life. Someone once said, "Challenges that are bigger than men, make men bigger."

Joshua Chamberlain had many talents. A professor from Maine, a trained theologian and a man of words, but he had not been trained to soldier. Unless you are a student of the American Civil War, or saw the movie "*Gettysburg,*" you may not recognize his name.

Later, he received the Congressional Medal of Honor and attained the rank of Brigadier General in the Union Army. He served as President of Bowdoin College and four terms as Governor of Maine.

But, on July 2, 1863, he found himself in the right place, at the right time. He had the responsibility and made the courageous decision that may have won the Battle of Gettysburg for the Union.

Lieutenant Colonel Chamberlain commanded the 20th Maine regiment. Their orders commanded them to hold the left flank of the Union line. The place, unknown then, but renowned now: Little Round Top.

If the Confederate troops had outflanked Chamberlain's men, the results of the battle might have been totally different. Possibly, even the outcome of the war and/or the election of 1864 would have changed.

The Confederates repeatedly advanced up the hill. They inflicted numerous casualties on Chamberlain's unit and suffered even more. But, they valiantly continued their advance. At one point, they progressed to within ten steps of the Union line. As both sides neared exhaustion of men, energy and ammunition, Chamberlain knew his command faced mortal peril. He must act with audacity or all would be lost.

While preparing for the next withering attack, Chamberlain gave the order that no one on either side expected. Charge!

The 20th Maine stormed down the hill. They won the day and have been a legend to military historians since.

Chamberlain displayed courage evidenced by few men. He led with confidence. His valor changed his life forever and the lives of untold others.

Joshua Chamberlain spoke at the dedication of the monument to the 20th Maine in 1886. He remarked, "The inspiration of a noble cause involving human interests wide and far, enables men to do things they did not dream themselves capable of before, and which they were not capable of alone. The consciousness of belonging, vitally to something beyond individuality; of being part of a personality that reaches we know not where, in space and in time, greatens the heart to the limits of the soul's ideal."[1]

Questions to ask yourself: What challenge do you face today? What goal of yours can you accomplish in the future by overcoming this challenge today? Who can help you in your effort? Is your dream worth the price you may have to pay to achieve it? Are you willing to step out of your comfort zone in the attempt to achieve it?

Principle Four

THE VALUE OF MONEY

When I was eleven, I received an allowance each week for the tasks my parents assigned me. However, there is a different dynamic involved when you are receiving money from mom and dad versus being paid by people with whom you have a strictly business relationship.

My paper route offered my first opportunity to work for a business and earn an income from those efforts. My net income each week, from delivering the paper, amounted to $6. This equated to less than $1 per day if everything went according to plan.

One of the first lessons I learned about my weekly income was that I had no guarantee to receive it. If I didn't succeed in collecting from a customer, the amount I didn't collect directly lowered my weekly income. In other words, if one customer didn't pay their weekly $.70 subscription fee, I would only earn $5.30. How many people, even as adults, put their income at such risk? Not many. I quickly realized that I could be the best deliverer of papers in the world, but if I could not reliably collect the subscription fees, I wouldn't make money.

I also realized that if I increased the number of customers I served, it would have a direct impact on increasing my income. This meant not only soliciting new customers, but also pleasing my existing customers to minimize any possibility that they might discontinue their subscription. Again, I had the opportunity to directly impact my income in a way that most adults never experience. This lesson benefited my adult career by teaching me **the importance of putting the customer first.** In reality, they paid me for my efforts.

Next, I began to comprehend the cost and value of items I desired because I learned what it took to earn my money. I learned that a relationship existed between my time and the "things" that I wanted. I could easily calculate how long I would have to work for a candy bar, soda, or a toy and then decide if I would buy it or save my money for a later time.

In addition, my parents taught me an additional lesson about money when they made me "put some skin into the game," as the saying goes. Instead of giving me what I asked for when I asked for it, they begin to include me in the decision process and requested my financial contribution for the things I thought I had to have. In a very short time, things I thought I couldn't live without became luxuries that would be nice to have, but not having them would not jeopardize my happiness. What began as making a choice to buy or not to buy candy evolved into more complicated items as I grew older.

The cost of the first car transaction I experienced involved a 50-50 split with my parents. My attitude toward that transaction could have been predicted from the lessons my parents and my very first job taught me. I appreciated my parents helping me to buy a car, instead of expecting them to buy one for me. Also, instead of feeling depressed because I didn't get a brand new, fancy car, my good, used car made me very happy. It is amazing how we all look at things differently if we have to directly pay for them rather than not having any sort of personal financial investment.

Finally, the culmination of the lessons above began to help me think about what something costs in a longer time frame, not just the price to purchase an item. This benefited me greatly later when I began thinking about cars. It isn't only the price to buy the car that must be considered, but also the costs for gas, insurance, and maintenance. It doesn't do you any good to buy something if you can't afford to keep it and it doesn't fit into your overall budget. While I didn't have any items of this complexity to buy at the age of eleven, each of the earlier-mentioned steps served as prerequisites for preparing me to make more detailed and important financial decisions.

Many things come naturally to a child, but one that does not is that children do not understand the value of money. My daughter is a perfect illustration. When she sees something she wants, she confidently states, "*I want that,*" without any regard to its cost or value. All she knows, or cares about, is that she wants something and she wants it NOW! We have already begun to teach her to consider what an item she desires costs and to give her choices from which to decide. It hasn't taken long to affect her decision making positively for her long-term benefit. She impressed me recently when she decided to spend some of the money she had saved in her piggy-bank for a nice dress instead of a toy.

While the behavior of my six-year-old daughter is understandable because of her age, there are many adults who act as she does. For some reason, they have not matured in their understanding of how money is earned, the cost of goods they desire, and the relationship of how long they must work in order to earn the money to buy them.

Additionally, it is insightful to observe people who have control over "other people's money" and how they treat it differently than their own. I have been amazed to watch people I have worked with who believe that no one will notice their actions. An example is that they will spend company money for lavish meals, but never do so with their own money. If you treat other people's money like you would treat your own, you will be a better steward and minimize the risk of making a bad judgment. You will also earn opportunities of additional responsibility; because you will have demonstrated your reliability with the opportunities you have been given. The people I described above sometimes lost opportunities because of the inconsistent way they handled company money compared to their own. They realized a much greater loss than the small amount of benefit they gained, and more importantly, they discovered their reputations irrevocably harmed. After learning the value of, and how to handle, your own money, you will also reveal your character in how you handle other people's money.

Few people today are unfamiliar with Wal-Mart. But, it hasn't always been that way. In the early 1960's, few people knew Wal-Mart and Sam Walton.

Born and raised with modest means, Sam learned the values that enabled him to build one of the largest retailers in the world. Those principles, which still guide the company after Sam's death, continue to make it successful.

Sam learned early the value of a dollar, of work, and of contributing to his family. He knew that to be successful long term, you had to be a giver and not a taker in any endeavor.

Sam recalled, "We learned how much hard work it took to get your hands on a dollar, and that when you did it was worth something."[1]

Strong principles, hard work, and teamwork have fueled the growth of the Wal-Mart Empire.

After becoming one of the wealthiest men in the world, most would not have recognized Sam's success by looking at him. He continued to drive an older model pick-up, which often carried dogs, as well as people. He didn't change his dress or lifestyle. He continued working as hard, after achieving financial independence, as he did in his effort to build his business.

Sam Walton's life showed him to be a rare individual. His preoccupation with delivering value to his customers, and positive treatment of his employees, resulted in success and respect beyond his imagination. As he said so well, "Every time Wal-Mart spends one dollar foolishly, it comes right out of our customer's pockets. Every time we save them a dollar that puts us one step ahead of the competition, which is where we always plan to be."[2] Sam Walton knew the value of money, and treated his customer's and stockholders money as he treated his own. His legacy continues to touch large numbers of people by providing more than just low prices on consumer items.

Questions to ask yourself: Do you know what something really costs? Do you respect and treat others money as responsibly as you do your own? Is your reputation and trustworthiness important to you?

Principle Five

THE BENEFIT OF DEFERRED GRATIFICATION

Because I now had a job, I realized that I would earn money every week. I had no direct expenses. I lived the dream of excess cash that most of us aren't able to return to after we become an adult. What would I do every week with $6?

Like all kids, I focused on candy, toys, and entertainment. However, I soon discovered two very important things. First, it didn't take long to get my fill of candy, toys, and entertainment available at that time. And, more importantly, acquiring more of these things didn't make me happier. After I spent all of my money, it occurred to me that I didn't have anything to show for it. In addition, I didn't have any extra money available if I decided I wanted to buy a more important item.

While my parents tried to teach me about saving money, the benefits didn't make sense to me until I learned about the value of money and began to think beyond the moment and the money that I had in my pocket.

As I considered these issues, my parents helped me discover a way to have fun, save money and learn the benefits of deferred gratification. Because I collected fees weekly from my paper route customers, I received and had to make change. My parents showed me the different types of coins, and that some of the ones I received actually had a value greater than the amount of the coin itself. I couldn't believe it. I earned money, and sometimes people paid me in money that turned out to be worth more by saving it than it would have been to spend it.

In the 1960's and 1970's, you could regularly receive valuable coins from your customers, because coin collecting was not as prevalent as it is today. I would look at every coin after I received it to see if it might be a collectable. If so, I would not give it away in change to the next customer or pay for my papers with it. Indian head pennies, Buffalo nickels, and Liberty dimes were among the gems I uncovered. The discovery of a rare 1909-penny increased my enthusiasm. When I returned home after collecting subscription fees, I would immediately sort the change and inspect it again for its value. I quickly had a growing collection.

I felt exhilarated as I discovered a rare coin. I have to believe the feeling is similar to finding a buried treasure. I found myself spending less money on consumable items, and putting more coins into my collection. I reasoned that, if I could locate valuable coins in the payments from my customers, valuable coins could probably be found in other change as well. I then began exchanging some of my income for rolls of coins from the bank. As I suspected, sorting through rolls of coins seemed like sifting for gold. It seemed as if in every roll, I discovered nuggets worth saving. As I collected more coins, I had more and more fun. I even motivated my grandmother to begin collecting coins. I still look for collectable coins, but it is much rarer to find them in circulation today.

Another benefit to discovering that I didn't have to spend all of my money is that I learned the benefit of saving money for a "rainy day." Having money set aside for financial emergencies made those emergencies less stressful than they otherwise would be. Some years later, I suffered a serious financial challenge. My savings provided me with a way to solve the issue. Why is it that we don't expect our elected officials or today's corporate leaders to live by this principle? It is interesting to note that for most of my life, when I lived by this belief, I have had financial success and security. But, during the brief period where I succumbed to the temptation of leveraging my financial resources to the maximum, I suffered my greatest financial reversal. When the real estate crash struck Texas in the mid 1980's, I owned four pieces of rental real estate. Because of my excessive leverage, I found myself forced to spend my entire savings and disposable income in a three-year futile effort to preserve my ownership.

Today, my wife and I work to teach our daughter these age-old lessons. While in its earliest stages, we have successfully taught Elizabeth that she *can* earn money for certain activities, such as learning the spelling lessons Laura is teaching her, helping out at home, or being good. We gave Elizabeth a see-through piggy bank to put the quarters in as she earns them. The first major purchase she desired ended up being a scooter like the other kids in the neighborhood had. Laura told her that when she had $10 in her piggybank, we would go to the store and she could buy that scooter. Periodically, Laura and Elizabeth would take out the coins and count them to see how much of her goal she had saved. After a few months, she finally had $10 in the bank and Elizabeth shouted with joy. We asked her what she wanted, and she replied sharply, "a scooter," as if she was surprised we didn't already know. Laura and I felt proud to see her maintain the desire for her prize for an extended period of time, and to learn that you didn't just walk into the store and leave with what you wanted without paying a price.

Deferred gratification is another characteristic I've learned is not inherent in people. Our society is especially challenged as seductive advertising constantly bombards us. We are used to buying food without having to leave our car, learn instantly about any subject via the Internet, see worldwide news as it occurs via satellite broadcasts and have the opportunity to become rich instantly by winning the lottery or a lawsuit. Easy credit and cultural norms have young people buying whatever they want, the moment they feel the desire. And today, Americans carry billions of dollars in credit card debt, which has increased substantially in the last 30 years. If these individuals have not had good training or experiences, it could be easy to fall into financial trouble.

The Benefit of Deferred Gratification 51

In every decision to spend money, we can choose to buy an item today, or save our money and be able to buy something else in the future or save for our retirement. In addition, if we can earn interest income from the money that we don't spend, we will have more money to spend on a future date. For example, think of an item that costs $10. What does it cost you to spend it, and not have the $10, plus earnings, for something else in the future? If you had $12 in the future, your original $10 plus earnings over time, could you acquire something of value that others without the money at that time couldn't? One illustration is that if you saved $ 1,000 per year for thirty years and were able to earn 5% interest per year, the resulting sum would be $ 69,760. If you save more, and or earn more, you can add to your results.

America produced a generation that grew up during the Great Depression of the 1930's and attained adulthood during World War II. They have become known as "The Greatest Generation."

Financial hardship and adversity occurred frequently during the depression. Necessity forced people to focus on getting by day-to-day and helping each other. The war threatened the life and liberty of the United States and its citizens. Again, people put family and country ahead of self.

This selfless group of Americans deferred their personal desires and goals, without dissent, until the economy recovered and victory in the war resulted. Only then, did those marvelous men and women concentrate on pursuing their own interests. Many of them realized tremendous success and happiness, which would not have been possible if they had not sacrificed their personal interests earlier. My parents are part of that generation. I appreciate their sacrifice, and that of all of their contemporaries, which contributed to the quality of life that I have been privileged to enjoy.

In *The Greatest Generation,* Tom Brokaw wrote, "They stayed true to their values of personal responsibility, duty, honor, and faith."[1] They serve as an example that every American should desire to emulate.

Texas during the 1980's reinforced this principle. A tremendous real estate crash happened. Depressed prices and unbelievable opportunities appeared simultaneously. To take advantage of those seldom-seen bargains, one had to have cash. Those who had capital and saw the magnitude of the deals available, prospered. Those who understood the unique market situation, but could not access cash, could merely watch those short-lived opportunities pass them by.

If you continually borrow money, and spend an increasing amount of your money on interest charges, what are you sacrificing in future goods to have a smaller amount of goods today? We each have the freedom and responsibility to decide how we will use our hard-earned money. With the perspective of many years of life, I can positively see the benefits people derive from deferring their gratification. I also see examples of the shortsightedness of people who succumb to spending everything they have and more and the stress and dependence that result from their limited vision.

Principle Six

Admit Your Mistakes and People Will Usually Forgive You

When nice weather presented itself, I would ride my bicycle and throw the newspapers I delivered onto the front porch of my customers. This approach is regrettably foreign to us today, but it was the standard practice until adults began throwing newspapers from their car window. It didn't take long to develop the proper skill to throw the paper to its target and, after a while, it became second nature. On one particular afternoon, I rode my bicycle and had almost completed my route when I threw a paper that changed that day and my life.

As I rode past the house, I heard the loud and distinctive sound of breaking glass. I immediately stopped my bike and looked over my shoulder. To my horror, the glass storm door had broken. Partially leaning out of it, the newspaper that I had just thrown protruded. My mind began working feverishly thinking, "What should I do?" The answer should have been apparent, but it came too slowly to my young mind. My fear of punishment wrestled with my desire to do the right thing.

After a few moments, but before anyone came to the door, I gathered my senses and decided that I had to go to the door and admit my mistake. I'm not quite sure if my choice came about because of my being smart, courageous, or from resigning myself that I couldn't get away with it. Whatever the reason, the right choice followed.

As the lady of the house answered the door, I was extremely nervous. While I'm sure she could tell what had happened with a brief glance, I admitted that I had accidentally broken her glass when I threw the paper. I offered to pay for the glass, knowing that it probably cost more than I made in a week. She thanked me for admitting my mistake and for stopping to come to the door and tell her about it.

Then, to my surprise, she said that I wouldn't have to pay to fix the glass. My heart beat so fast with excitement that I almost missed the most important point. She added that she didn't ask me to replace the glass because I had stopped and admitted my mistake. After a few more exchanges, I eagerly jumped back on my bike to complete my route that day.

I wonder if that nameless lady knows how much she impacted my future. With her willingness to forgive me and pay for my mistake, she demonstrated that if you admit to your mistakes, people will usually forgive you. This woman, independently, reinforced what my parents had worked to teach me. This greatly increased their credibility with me.

Later, I realized that the opposite of what had happened could have easily occurred. If I had run away, in a short time, I would have been discovered to be the one who broke the glass. If I had not owned up to my mistake, I would have had to pay for the glass, which would have hurt me financially in the short run, but more importantly, I would have missed the opportunity to learn a valuable lesson.

My parents worked to instill the importance of admitting my mistakes in me as part of my growing up. But, my first non-family episode proved their point. It changed my opinion of adults, my parents, and touched my future experiences.

While I have had other incidents that illustrate this lesson, there is one that stands out in my professional career that is worth sharing with you. Again, I faced a stark choice: blame someone else for a problem or admit my own responsibility.

As a young sales rep, I sold microfilm systems to businesses. My biggest customer was a large insurance company. I inherited the account when my friend and co-worker, C.B. Huchingson, who had originally sold it, had been promoted to sales manager. Needless to say, the customer had no reason to trust me or find anything I said credible, because I had not proven myself. I knew, though, that this account could provide me with more than one fourth of my yearly quota and income, so I eagerly worked to take care of their needs.

Shortly after taking over the account, I took an order for a large supply item. Excitement overcame me, because I would soon reap the reward from this large customer. In a few days, when I visited the account, I was dismayed to discover that I had ordered the wrong product. Again, I quickly considered my options.

When my contact asked me what had happened, the temptation to blame the problem on "the computer" or "sales administration" tempted me. But, based on my previously stated experience and other similar ones, I refrained from making an excuse. I stated, "It is my fault because I ordered the wrong product." She thanked me for admitting the mistake and I loaded up the incorrect product to take to my office, while placing an order for the correct product. It took me a long time to sell the entire incorrectly ordered product because of the volume. And, every time I looked at it stacked in my office, it reminded me of my mistake.

This time, I didn't immediately notice the benefit of admitting my error. I just knew the correct product showed up and I began a routine of taking good care of my customer.

Some time later, this company showed interested in a product we offered and they looked at my offering as well as a competitor's. It concerned me, because the competitive product had excellent features and a price lower than my offering. To my pleasant surprise, I received the order. I wondered, "Why did they buy this from me?"

The answer to my question came shortly after the new equipment had been installed. Because I had a good relationship and communication with my customer, I asked them why they bought this product from me. They told me candidly that I received their business because they knew they could trust me and that I would tell them the truth whether the news would be good or bad. I served that customer for many years and I received all of their business. Sometimes, my product offer might be the best, but my honesty was what made the difference in their decisions to buy my products.

Again, I not only benefited financially from admitting my mistake, but I saw that **PEOPLE VALUE HONESTY OVER ANYTHING ELSE IN A RELATIONSHIP.**

Because people so often avoid taking responsibility, and look to place blame on someone else, people who are responsible and admit their failings are highly esteemed. If someone knows that you will be honest whether you are right or wrong, and will do what is right, you will experience many more benefits than you will suffer from the pain of admitting your mistakes.

I had never heard of David Marshall Williams until I saw his story in the 1952 movie, "*Carbine Williams,*" which starred Jimmy Stewart. His achievements hastened the victory in World War II and perhaps made many of our lives possible today. But if you looked at his early life, you would never surmise that he would contribute anything positive to the world.

Marsh Williams grew up in a modest environment. During Prohibition, he discovered that he could earn more money bootlegging alcohol than by any honest means. During a raid by the authorities, a federal agent died by gunshot. No one knew exactly who fired the shot, but it fell upon Marsh, as the best shot there, to answer for it. His pride would not permit him to hurt his friends and he refused to testify against them.

A plea agreement with the prosecutor and judge for a three-year sentence had Williams prepared to atone for the crime. Then, another judge substituted for the original trial judge and he refused to honor the plea agreement. Williams ended up sentenced to 30 years hard labor and became embittered toward the law and authority.

Prison life demanded discipline and hard work on a chain gang. Marsh defiantly stood up to the guards and warden. He frequently received punishment and spent considerable time in solitary confinement. No one had lasted more than seven days in solitary, but Marsh spent thirty days there once before the prison doctor insisted upon his release. The warden curiously wanted to know how he survived so long in such horrific conditions.

Marsh said that during his confinement, he thought of an idea for a new rifle and designed it in his mind. The thought of an incarcerated prisoner drawing guns would elicit an immediate and strong disciplinary response in virtually every situation. In spite of his toughness, the warden could see hope for Williams under his rugged exterior. He saw past the risk, and decided that this project might give Williams the hope to respond to authority and discipline.

After many discussions amongst prison officials, Marsh received permission to use a file and was given the opportunity to build a gun from his design. He constructed the stock out of a fence post and the barrel out of a tractor axle.

Given a second chance, he changed his attitude. Marsh began to see that if he cooperated with officials, he could earn opportunities and eventually his freedom.

It took him six years to finish his rifle! Upon its completion, a bold suggestion that Williams be allowed to test fire the weapon initiated further concern and discussions. But, the authorities allowed him to proceed.

He became consumed with his passion to build a weapon that would be lighter, more reliable and would fire faster than any other rifle in use at the time. Based on his work, he received a contract with Winchester.

The first weapon he designed and patented eventually became the famous M-1 carbine. The impact it provided Allied soldiers to speed the victory and reduce casualties during World War II is unmistaken, but hard to numerically calculate.

David Marshall "Carbine" Williams eventually received a pardon from prison. He went on to successfully work in the weapons industry and secured 59 patents. Once he admitted his mistake, submitted to authority, and paid the price, he was given a second chance. He made many contributions which benefited his country.

There are many times in life that we are faced with the choice to avoid or face up to our mistakes. I don't know why, but it always appears that avoiding our mistakes will be easy and pain free. It seldom is. It is extremely rare that we can escape accepting responsibility. When we try to hide our mistakes, the cost is always higher than it would have been if we had initially admitted responsibility. Another way to illustrate this is with the expression, "take the easy way out." I believe it is an oxymoron because what appears as the "easy way out" is seldom easy or the way out.

Conversely, it always appears that if we confess our mistakes, the penalty will be severe. In fact, in every experience I have had, I have benefited from accepting my just responsibility. My closest relationships are with people whom I know will confess a mistake and they know I will forgive their mistake as they will forgive mine.

Principle Seven

THE QUALITY OF YOUR SERVICE MATTERS

My paper route in the cold Chicago weather gave me the opportunity to learn and practice several traits in order to provide my customers with the very best service possible. Some of them may seem obvious, but I learned during my career that the quality of service you deliver in your work matters greatly. And, as obvious as some of these truths are, the majority of people don't excel at all or most of them. As a result, if you practice these essential traits, you will deliver the highest quality service and you will stand out in any endeavor that you attempt.

The most important thing that my newspaper customers expected from me was that I would deliver their paper at a time they pre-determined in their mind. In blunt words, **SHOW UP ON TIME!** It seems so simple, but many people don't appreciate its importance. It didn't matter when *I* thought the papers should be delivered to the customer, but when *they* expected to receive the paper. In our drive-thru, fast-food world, I find myself expecting certain levels of service. If a provider doesn't deliver to my expectations, I have a negative reaction, and go elsewhere. The subscribers to the newspaper I delivered had the same expectations from my service.

Today, a friend of mine is so used to me showing up on time for our meetings that, if I show up a few minutes late, he checks to see if he has made a mistake regarding our appointment. As you can see, I have developed a reputation with him of being on time. Conversely, if I always showed up late, he would be unhappy that I arrived late, and that may have a negative impact on our meeting and our relationship.

The second trait required in order to provide superior quality service is to **DO WHAT YOU SAY**. This is where you have the opportunity to earn your customer's trust and influence their expectations of you. If your customer expects you to deliver a service at 9:00 am, but you can't for whatever reason, you must communicate what you will do. If my paper customer expected the paper on his or her doorstep by 2:00 pm on a school day, I could not meet his or her expectation. I could not get out of school in time or receive my papers by that time. I needed to communicate the time I could deliver his or her paper and then do what I said.

Next, I discovered an important trait in committing yourself to your customer. It is always better to *UNDER* **PROMISE AND** *OVER* **DELIVER** than it is to *over* promise and *under* deliver. Despite pressure from a customer to deliver his or her paper by 2:00 pm, it would be better to tell them that I could have it to them by 4:00 pm because of my school schedule. Then it would be a happy surprise to have the paper there by 3:45 pm instead of promising it by 2:00 pm, but not delivering it until 3:45 pm. Despite the paper being delivered at exactly the same time in both examples, the customer would be happier in the first scenario. As you can see, the opportunity to satisfy my customer was based on my response and my management of their expectation. Don't let the "pressure to please" overcome your common sense to tell the truth! While you will feel better for a very short time after telling someone what they want to hear, you will suffer a loss of respect, for a much longer time, if you can not deliver something that you promised. You may even lose the relationship.

Another trait that is mandatory in order to deliver the highest quality service is to **BE HONEST** in all of your dealings. While addressed in chapter six, it is relevant to this chapter, and crucial enough to emphasize here. While you may think that you can get by with a "little white lie," you can't. And the person you think you're fooling probably knows what is going on. I discussed my initial experience with this in the previous chapter. It always amazed me that some sales reps, whom I supervised, tried to fudge on their expense reports and believed that they got away with a few dollars here and there. What they did became obvious, and they always hurt themselves in the long run. They missed being considered for opportunities that would have benefited them far greater than the few dollars they added to their expense reports. On the other hand, employees who are honest and forthright earn additional opportunities and the benefit of the doubt in any situation, which is far more beneficial to their success.

As I grew up, my parents and grandparents never missed an opportunity to tell me how important it is to do your very best in anything that you attempt. This included school, sports, work and any other activity.

I did just fine in most areas. But, I wish I had discovered earlier that **EVERYTHING YOU DO TODAY WILL IMPACT YOUR FUTURE.** Recognizing that fact as early as possible and dedicating yourself to adopt it as your philosophy and creed will benefit your entire life.

We select doctors, painters, plumbers, lawyers and other service providers by the same characteristics that I have emphasized above. If they provide a superior service, we will pay more, wait longer, and trust their recommendations. Conversely, if their service is substandard, we will have a low threshold of tolerance before we search for another provider.

I will cite an example of poor service with an additional twist. Two associates and I traveled on a business trip to Birmingham, England in 2003. Upon completion of a fine meal, with spotty service, I presented my credit card to pay the check.

When the waitress returned the bill to me, it looked similar to what I had grown accustomed to in the United States. At the top, the food and beverage had been added and listed as the sub-total. A line for a tip or gratuity and then a line for the total followed.

But, there was a stark difference in what I had presented to me, and what I received in restaurants back home. The server had drawn a diagonal line through the tip space and had handwritten the sub-total amount into the total field.

I had never seen this before. My curiosity overcame me and I had to ask the server what it meant. I asked, "Are you not interested in receiving a tip?" She frankly replied, "Due to taxes, I will only see about 40% of the tip you would give me. And, because of the complications of the paperwork I will have to complete for my taxes, it is not worth receiving a tip." She restated that she would prefer not to receive a tip.

Then it became very clear to me. The poor quality service we received correlated in direct proportion to the server's lack of motivation to earn additional money for providing superior service.

In the United States, servers rely on tips for the majority of their income. It is in their best interest to provide the highest quality service in order to reap the largest gratuity possible. It is also important to deliver exceptional service to attract repeat and long-term patronage of their clients.

The only location where we saw exceptional service happened at a restaurant in London, which had a U.S. theme and had Americans managing it. I don't know what they did to produce the excellent service that we experienced, but my bet is that they provided incentives to motivate their employees.

It is illustrative to see the difference between the U.S.,

which has a market-driven economy, and the U.K., which is more socialized. This example is from a micro perspective, but if you expand it to a macro view, you can see why productivity, quantity and quality of products and services, and the standard of living are higher in the U.S. when compared to more socialized countries. On the surface, the countries and people look very similar. But, it doesn't take long to see the effects of the illustration above on a larger scale.

People will respond and trade their time and effort when they are given an opportunity to receive something that they want for their sacrifice. It may be additional income, recognition, self-satisfaction or anything else they personally desire. On the other hand, when they see that, regardless of their effort, they will not be rewarded, they will not expend their energy beyond the minimal requirement.

I am very grateful to live in a country that permits, and encourages, people to work hard and gives them the incentive and reward for their efforts. We can be rewarded short and/or long term, monetarily and/or non-monetarily, materially and/or non-materially.

Another perspective is to **ALWAYS THINK LIKE THE BUYER OF A SERVICE WHEN YOU ARE THE PROVIDER**. What would impress you as excellent service? How can you set yourself apart compared to your competition? Are you willing to differentiate yourself in order to demonstrate that you are the best choice available?

There is a tendency, in any endeavor, to work hard until a certain level of performance is achieved and then level off and perform at that level for an extended period of time. Another way to describe this is someone reaching his or her comfort level and then coasting. Accepting that you have achieved your best, and being satisfied to the point of not diligently working to continually improve yourself, is a disservice to those you serve and also to yourself.

THERE IS ALWAYS SOMETHING YOU CAN DO TO IMPROVE WHAT YOU ARE DOING. As H.E. Butt of the H.E.B. grocery chain in Texas said, "The mortal enemy of best is good." If we are satisfied with a good effort, why should we be surprised if we lose an opportunity to serve a customer who may find a source who delivers a best effort? It is easy to rationalize that our competitor provided the service for a lower price, an inferior product, or some other unconquerable reason, but sometimes it could be because someone else is doing a better job. If you are focused on being the best at what you do, and delivering superior service, you will be amazed at the results you achieve compared to those who are comfortable delivering a good service.

It is also easy to rationalize that your performance is okay because you are performing at the same level as others. That should not be the yardstick we measure ourselves against! What is important is how we perform and deliver our service compared to our ability. As I explain to my sales representatives, one measurement of your success is against your quota and the other is where you stand in the rankings of all the other sales reps. Quota is the assigned dollars of sales a person has to achieve to satisfactorily do their job. If everyone is more than

100% of an assigned number, being 100% isn't successful if you're at the bottom of the list which ranks all of the salespeople. Conversely if you're at 85% of your assigned number, but you are at the top of the list ranking all of the salespeople, you are more successful, even though you should not be satisfied without achieving your assigned quota number.

The expression, "Not doing more than the average is what keeps the average down," illustrates this. Some people will try to persuade you to not perform better because you may make them look bad. You are the loser when you fall for that line of reasoning and abandon the opportunity to achieve your dreams. You will be like the fellow who tried to climb the ladder out of the pit. He never made it because his fellow inhabitants kept pulling him back down by his legs as he climbed. This illustration is described as the "crab effect." You have the ability to set your own standards of effort and to try your very best to achieve them. No one should be able to deter you from attempting great things in pursuit of your dreams.

What does quality of service have to do with you attempting your dreams? Benjamin Franklin said, "When you're good to others, you're best to yourself." When you are giving your best effort in serving others, and working to improve yourself, you will stand out like a beacon from a lighthouse on a dark night. You will be recognized for the different level of service you provide and doors of opportunity will be open to you. This could be better jobs, important contacts, friendships and other benefits that will help you in the quest of your dreams.

Principle Eight

PATIENCE MUST BE LEARNED

My additional role as a young employee provided an early test of my temperament and a real world experience that gave me the opportunity to learn to be more patient. Human nature is the same now as I experienced it at eleven. In fact, it hasn't changed in thousands of years. When I deal with my co-workers and customers today, I see the same behavior as I did when I had my paper route. I could not control things the newspaper did, the actions of my customers, the weather, or many other things involved in accomplishing my daily responsibility. Now, as then, how we respond to the activities of those we deal with is important to our overall success. Oftentimes, we have to do things we don't want to do in ways we don't want to do them, but they are the right things to do for all the parties involved.

Every day, I waited on my papers to be delivered to me before I could begin the process to deliver them. I could not control whether they would show up when I expected them or if they would be in good condition. Both of these factors significantly affected the quality of service I provided my customers. But, I could control how I responded to a delay in receiving the papers or if I received the papers wet or damaged. If I responded negatively, it could negatively affect the rest of the day for my family, my customers and me.

If I could have had my way, all of my customers would have paid me with the exact change every Thursday when I began my weekly effort to collect their subscription money. Unfortunately, it never transpired that easily. Sometimes, I would have to ask for the money on Thursday, Friday and Saturday before I received it. My youth made it difficult to know if someone might have a situation that prevented him or her from paying me on Thursday, so I asked every day for his or her payment. I did learn that no matter how badly I wanted to collect the money, I could do nothing more than ask. But, if I let it bother me that someone delayed his or her payment, I would suffer more than he or she did!

Years later, I owned some rental real estate and had some extremely negative experiences trying to collect rent. In spite of the heartache and financial loss I suffered, I did not allow the experience to sour my outlook on life. My early lessons on collecting money and the patience it taught me benefited me during this otherwise forgetful experience.

Some people who know me will laugh at this characteristic because I may not have exhibited patience to them. **Like many other characteristics essential to our success and happiness,**

patience is one that we are not born with, but hopefully will learn through the rigors of experience. I am grateful that I am more patient now than I used to be, but I hope to become more patient in the future.

I was blessed to have total support from my parents and younger brother, Jerry, in order to fulfill my delivery responsibilities. When my papers arrived late, Jerry would pitch in so that I could make the deliveries on time. When the weather deteriorated, my mother or father would drive me in order to make the job easier and to help me meet my obligation. I appreciated the help and I don't remember taking it for granted. It can be easy to receive help to the point of believing that you are entitled to it and that it should come on your terms.

I discovered times then, and there are times now, when we have people willing to help us, but we must be patient to wait for our help to arrive. If we proceed without waiting for our expected help, we may move faster, but not accomplish what we set out to do. In chapter 13, I will discuss an example from my paper route that could have been tragic, but I am thankful it didn't turn out that way.

One of the things that I enjoy doing in my business travel is observing other travelers deal with the frustration of cancelled or delayed flights. It is instructive to watch people throw a tantrum so they can get home on time to watch a television show or for some similarly unimportant reason, which they deem more urgent than their travel safety. It is most often the less experienced traveler who exhibits anger at an airline because they won't fly through a snowstorm or bad weather. The experienced traveler understands that every airline would face the same delay.

One of the advantages of maturity is that you realize that things are often not as urgent as they seem. Once we experience and recognize that, we give ourselves the luxury of being more patient in a situation, which enables us to respond better to it. We also can respond more thoughtfully and less emotionally, which again permits us to make better long-term choices. We become able to make our choices on our timetable and not the timetable of those who are pushing us for a response to meet their needs.

Born into a powerful family, and achieving greatness before the end of the 19th century, Sir Winston Churchill was arguably the finest political leader of the 20th century.

Long recognized for his determination and achievements during World War II, he may have been even more successful between 1932 and 1940. These are the years that William Manchester described in *Alone*, the second volume of a three-volume biography on Churchill.

After previous political and wartime successes, Churchill then faced his mid-life years with a series of setbacks between 1922 and 1940. He lost elections, his creditors doggedly pressured him for payment, his own political party rejected him, and he found himself cast out socially. It would have been easier to reflect on past achievements, and accept that his time in leadership had past. It would have been natural to focus on himself and his personal desires, but Churchill's style was not in reflecting and accepting, but in moving forward.

Churchill continually put his country ahead of his own interests. He alone stood up and spoke out against Hitler's advances and the timid response by British leadership.

During his time out of power, he wrote extensively, extended his network of contacts and allies, continued to serve in Parliament as a "back bencher" and prepared for his next leadership opportunity.

Upon his return as Prime Minister in 1940, Churchill displayed confidence and determination in his leadership of Great Britain against her enemies in World War II. He had been tested by his life experiences, which complimented his other strengths. Together, these traits enabled him to be the "steady hand" of leadership when other's hands trembled.

What price would the world have paid had Churchill focused on his needs instead of the needs of England during his time out of influence and power? The difference he made in our world then and today is incalculable. His exercise of patience, preparation and perspective delivered him and England through "their finest hour" during World War II.[1] His example is one of encouragement and hope.

Can you remember a time in your life where, had you been patient, you would have benefited? Have those experiences encouraged you to put things into a larger perspective than that of the moment? Are you more patient with others than you used to be? Patience, even after it is learned, must be exercised regularly to become a part of one's character.

Principle Nine

THERE IS SYNERGY IN TEAMWORK

Most of my customers never saw anyone from the newspaper except me. In fact, I contributed a small part to a large team. I always felt privileged to be able to interact with the customers because so many other, more critical members of the team, could not receive the affirmation of their efforts.

My family is another team that I played a part of as a paperboy. Even though the job had my name on it, I could not have succeeded without the support of my parents and brother. My brother, Jerry, would help me fold the papers and at times, accompany me on the deliveries. Occasionally, he would fill in for me. Sometimes during bad weather, my parents would drive me in the car, to make my job easier. It would have been much easier for them to allow me to fulfill my responsibilities without their assistance.

All of us have friends or family who periodically help us in our work efforts. Too often, we overlook those whose contributions and support make a difference in the results of our efforts. If we don't recognize, acknowledge and return the favor to our friends and family, we are the ones who will lose in the long run.

Participating in youth team sports, and other group activities, is a great preparation for working on a team. However, the dynamic of people earning money adds a dimension to the relationships and endeavor, which is missing from efforts where no money is involved.

The world of team sports is filled with individuals, many of whom have large egos who routinely put self ahead of team. With free agency, it is rare for an athlete to spend an entire career with a single team. The pursuit of money, fame, and a championship ring drives players to maximize their short-term opportunities.

Those facts make the achievement of the 1972 Miami Dolphins of the NFL stand out compared to contemporary teams. Their 17-0 record is remarkable because no team since has been able to complete an undefeated season. They won the Super Bowl VII and their defense posted three shutouts.

They amazed people with their performance because the team had no super-stars on their defensive squad at the time. They won over and over, and they did it because they played together.

The defensive players recognized that if they all worked together, they could succeed. And, if they succeeded, there would be ample credit for everyone. Later, football fans recognized many of the names. Nick Buoniconti eventually became enshrined into the NFL Hall of Fame.

According to Cbsportline.com, the "no-name defense" originated just before Super Bowl VI the prior season. Dallas Cowboys coach, Tom Landry, when asked to comment on the Dolphins defense said, "I can't recall their names." What a compliment to the eleven starters, other players and coaches of that team! They had only allowed 174 regular season points, and the opposing coach, a recognized defensive genius, could not recall the name any of their players.

While the Dolphins lost Super Bowl VI, they won not only Super Bowl VII, but Super Bowl VIII as well. The three-year record they achieved became the envy of the league. Their dedication to the team above the individual is an example worthy of everyone's emulation.

There is a tendency, for many people, to lose focus on the team aspect of their work, and submit to the illusion that without their effort, the business would not succeed. In reality, most team efforts require everyone on the team to fulfill their responsibilities in order to succeed. Still, it only takes one person not performing satisfactorily for the team to fail.

Another way to describe it is that the total effort of a team is greater than the sum of the individual contributions. That is the effect known as "synergy," as described by Stephen Covey in "*The Seven Habits of Highly Successful People.*"

In the 1980's, I fortunately belonged to the Austin, Texas chapter of the Junior Chamber of Commerce (Jaycees). It is a volunteer organization dedicated to serving the community and providing leadership training.

Our local organization had hundreds of members who came from varied backgrounds and possessed different goals. We came together though, with a common objective to give something back to our community.

Individually, we would have been able to accomplish little. However, our combined and accumulated efforts, we completed hundreds of projects that benefited tens of thousands of people. We contributed hundreds of thousands of dollars to charity. We saw lives changed and received national and international recognition for our efforts.

President John F. Kennedy said, "One man can make a difference, and every man should try." This happened when one of our members had the idea to conduct a charity golf tournament featuring professional football players and other celebrities. It would be patterned after one he witnessed in another city. He wanted to support the Muscular Dystrophy Association (MDA) because he had a close relative with the disease.

Our club seized their opportunity to make a difference. We rallied support from the community. Several months and innumerable man-hours later, the participants enjoyed a wonderful tournament. Unfortunately, we lost over $ 20,000.

Undeterred, we committed to try again. With a full year's planning and a tremendous amount of work, we had a more successful tournament. In addition, we retired the debt from the previous year and proudly made an $ 11,000 contribution to MDA.

Over the next five years, MDA received more than $240,000 in donations from the event. The tournament is now more than twenty years old and is still benefiting charity.

This success began because one individual had an idea and recruited others to labor at his side. The power of many in the attempt of a common goal and the synergy of that endeavor has and is making a vast difference in people's lives.

With rare exception, you will be part of a team in your many work experiences. As a result, developing interpersonal skills will benefit you and the team.

As team members, our first duty is to complete our responsibilities. A lot of people are satisfied with just doing their job and miss a grand opportunity for additional success. For those who look beyond their own responsibility, there is an opportunity to contribute more to the team's achievement. The person who is always looking to learn more, give more, pick up the slack wherever it may be, do whatever job will help the team triumph, will stand out like a full moon on a cloudless night. Those individuals will learn more, see doors of opportunity open for them, and impact many more people during their lives.

As Emerson said, "It is one of the most beautiful compensations of this life that no man can sincerely try to help another without helping himself." In other words, **pitch in and help your team and teammates, and you will benefit more than you can possibly contribute.** If it is clear to your team that you only care about yourself, you will not benefit. In order for this dynamic to work, you must sacrifice your own desires and work as hard as you can to help the team. If you do this, you will be rewarded beyond your efforts.

Zig Ziglar delivers the same message another way. He says, "You can get anything you want in life if you help enough other people to get what they want." Again, be a good teammate and your team will be more successful. Contribute more than you are responsible for and you will be rewarded often beyond your wildest dreams.

Principle Ten

THE BEST LEADERSHIP IS BY EXAMPLE

As a youngster, working part time, I didn't think very much about influencing others, but in hindsight, that's exactly what I did. Like it or not, my younger brother looked to me as an example. He not only supported and assisted my efforts, but also viewed the benefits I received. Other kids in the neighborhood, whom I didn't even know, might also have seen and been influenced, similar to the way my predecessor influenced me.

I didn't have a great opportunity to lead in my job as a paperboy, but I learned a lot about leadership. I saw how my parents used it as a teaching tool for me, how the people I worked for led by example and I saw, first hand, how my predecessor fulfilled the job requirements.

I learned how to do the job when everything went right, but more importantly, I saw and learned from others how to deal with adversity. Whether I received the papers late, faced challenging weather, or had difficulty collecting the subscription fees, I learned how to get the job done when things went wrong. These experiences helped me in business, civic and other activities later in life.

My good fortune is that my parents and grandparents taught me the merit of hard work and, by their example, reinforced the values they held so dearly. They instilled into me a sense of responsibility for things beyond myself at an early age.

Likewise, we have a neighbor boy named Marshall who has worked very hard, since his early teens, babysitting, and mowing lawns, among other things. He doesn't recognize how the younger children in the neighborhood look up to him or the positive example he has demonstrated. The children he has touched may not recognize it either, but it will enhance their lives.

There are an almost infinite number of philosophies of leadership, which are advocated, written about, taught and practiced. An individual could spend his or her entire life studying and exploring leadership and its nuances. My objective is not to discuss and compare philosophies, but to emphasize the implementation phase of leadership.

It doesn't matter how old you are, or what position you hold in society. You influence others by your actions, whether they are positive or negative. I said "actions" because they, and not your words, will reveal the results of your efforts. Ideally, your actions will mirror your words, but that isn't so with everyone. The old expression, "How can I hear what you say when what you do speaks so loudly?" illustrates the emphasis on action.

You cannot opt out of your opportunity and responsibility to positively impact others. Self-centered athletes and Hollywood types say that they don't want to be a role model for others because they want to be able to do anything they want without consequence. The truth is that they *are* role models, whether they like it or not. The question is what type of example will they offer to the public?

And so it is with leadership. We will provide an example in the way we exercise leadership, whether or not we choose. The question is do we lead by word or deed? The best leaders I have seen in my life lead by example. They aren't afraid to do what they ask others to do. They put the effort to achieve their goals above their personal desires. They recognize the message they communicate by their actions. These leaders succeed over time because time has validated this method of leadership. These leaders can weather a storm because their foundation is solid.

I also have had the misfortune to work with those who tried to lead without providing a positive example. They thought themselves above those whom they led and felt they could better spend their time on efforts they believed were more important. They either masked their ignorance of their responsibility to set an example or put their personal desires first. They did not recognize that they received disrespect and scorn by those they led. In the end, I have never seen someone be consistently successful whose actions did not mirror his or her words.

In good times, almost any leadership style may succeed. In the tough times, the difference in success and failure may be as little as the respect the leader is given by those whom he leads.

As I have had the opportunity to lead others in different capacities, I sometimes experienced difficulty persuading some individuals to do the things that would benefit them in the long run. The late coach of the Dallas Cowboys, Tom Landry, defined leadership this way: "Leadership is the ability to get people to do what they don't want to do, but what they need to do to become better."

Leadership, by its definition, says that we're going to take people where they may not have gone before. Thus, it requires people to venture away from their comfort zone, which they dislike. When a group doesn't want to venture into uncharted water, it requires a valiant leader to inspire them to move. In that situation, the leader who has the respect of those he leads, because of the example he has set, will have the reservoir of good will established that will help him move those who don't want to be moved.

Among the examples is Sam Houston. Before migrating to Texas, he had already served Tennessee as a congressman and governor. After 1836, he would serve twice as President of the Republic of Texas, and also as governor and U.S. Senator after Texas became a state.

But in the pivotal year of 1836, Houston commanded the small Texas Army and volunteers. For six long weeks he led the army in a strategic retreat, known as "The Runaway Scrape." It gave him time to prepare to fight Santa Anna and win independence for Texas. Many grumbled and disapproved of his tactics, but his reputation as a leader, and the fact that he traveled with his troops, experiencing all of their hardships, may have been the only thing that prevented a mutiny.

On April 21, 1836, outnumbered, but motivated, Texas forces decisively defeated the Mexican Army at the Battle of San Jacinto near present-day Houston. Selecting the unique location, directing the successful tactics and having the patience to wait for the right moment illustrated Houston's decisive leadership.

The reservoir of respect Houston commanded before the battle may have been the irreplaceable component, which resulted in Texas independence instead of just another failed revolution in the course of history. The leader who has not led by example will have the most difficult time because he has not proven to those he leads that he will be successful in the effort.

Contemporary society encourages "consensus" leadership, which is at odds with "leadership by example." It frowns on individual thought, spirited debate, voting against the group, and asserting views different than the "enlightened" majority, out of an almost fear of the results. Stifling different opinions is damaging to creativity, individual initiative and freedom of thought. Unchallenged, it can threaten progress and our way of life.

To realize personal growth, prosper long term and lead others, it is imperative to resist the temptation to fall into "groupthink." "Be sure you're right, then go ahead" is the motto identified with Alamo hero and statesman, Davy Crockett. If you do the right thing for the right reason, you may suffer in the short term, but you will succeed in the long run.

If you boldly step out in an effort, others will join and follow your lead. People are much more likely to join someone who makes the first move than they are to step out themselves. Years ago, a political debate occurred in my city to issue general obligation bonds to finance affordable housing units. While politically correct, many believed it financially irresponsible at the time because of the surplus of available housing in the private sector and the low rents available. If passed, it would have increased the housing supply, further reduced rents, and enlarged the financial damage people who owned rental property suffered at the time. Many spoke for it, but no one dared say anything against it. Seeing no one else standing up to decry the lack of reasoning of the proposal, I decided to speak against it at a city council meeting. After my presentation, I left the meeting and had several people seek me out who agreed with me, but who did not want to be the first person to speak against the matter. We banded together and I found myself leading the effort, which successfully defeated the proposition. This tremendous experience reinforced this lesson.

Another quote that I admire says, "Do not follow where the path may lead. Go instead where there is no path and leave a trail."

You will have opportunities in your life to influence and lead others. Questions to ask yourself: Will you set an example and ask others to follow it or will you sit in an ivory tower and expect others to follow your words? Will you have the courage to take risks and step into unfamiliar ground in order to achieve major success?

Principle Eleven

PERSIST IN THE FACE OF ADVERSITY

I encountered things fulfilling my duties as a paperboy that seemed difficult, if not impossible, at the time. In reality, though, they served as stepping stones. Successfully completing my responsibilities provided me with a foundation of confidence that has benefited me since that initial experience.

As I have previously mentioned, I found collecting the weekly subscription fee one of my most challenging responsibilities. Because, I perceived it as being an unpleasant task, I could have avoided it until late in the week. By doing that, however, I would have risked not collecting all of my money on a timely basis, which would have resulted in negative response from my manager. Instead, I discovered that if I started early, in an effort to complete the unappealing chore, I would be more successful and not experience the problems I feared.

This experience has been reinforced throughout my life. The anticipation of something, which you don't want to do, is worse, in nearly every instance, than actually doing that task.

My list of responsibilities also included soliciting new customers. I faced that task with anxiety. Overcoming my hesitancy helped me to succeed and provided me with a confidence I have relied upon in my sales and business career.

As I mentioned in Chapter 3, I lost some of the money I had collected one day while riding my bicycle home. Crestfallen, I fortunately later realized the importance of protecting my money. My lesson cost little compared to the small amount of actual cash I lost.

I had to deliver the papers, collect the subscription fees, and solicit new customers to be successful. It would have been an easier path to quit, or to have delayed or avoided the other areas. A favorite quote of mine says, "Obstacles are those frightful things you see when you take your eyes off of the goal." Because I focused on being successful at my total responsibility, I persevered through the parts of the job that I didn't care for in order to succeed at the total job. This lesson proved essential, because I have never found a job that didn't require me to complete some duties that I wish I didn't have to do.

In hindsight, it benefited me as a child to experience early on that I would not always have everything I desired. Every episode of adversity I have experienced, while painful at the moment, has positively affected my life.

It is easy to make money in the stock market when it is steadily rising. It is easy to overachieve your sales quota when you have no competition. And life is easy when everything goes the way in which you want it. I see this demonstrated daily with my young daughter. She is a very sweet child, but occasionally, when she doesn't get things her way, she will throw a tantrum in an effort to have things the way she would like them. Oh, for life to be that simple!

In reality, life will be difficult at times. Everyone, at one time or another, comes face to face with unpleasant situations. **THE TRUE TEST OF A MAN'S CHARACTER IS HOW HE RESPONDS TO ADVERSITY.** People experience not getting their own way, rejection, trauma, loss and/or other challenges over the course of their lives. When we're young, the natural response to not getting our way, or encountering a problem, is to cry. As we mature, we discover that no matter what our response is, we cannot always manipulate the situation in our favor. When we know that we have to live with an adverse situation, that we can't change, we are forced to learn alternative reactions. One of the signs and advantages of maturing is gaining the experience and confidence to respond to negative experiences.

Our comeback from adversity will determine the way it will impact our future. Will we quit at the first sign of trouble or will we stand and face it in an effort to succeed? If we quit, we may gain a momentary respite, but we will forgo the opportunity to overcome and learn from it. If we face it, we may not succeed, but we will almost, without exception, gain invaluable lessons and confidence in preparation to meet future challenges.

Most of us feel that we face more than our share of trials and tribulations in life. In reality, we are privileged when compared to those who face true adversity. Paul Alexander of Dallas, Texas is one of those individuals. His story of personal triumph should inspire us all to look at life and live it with a different attitude.

Paul earned admission to the bar as an attorney-at-law in Texas in 1986. It is unusual for someone becoming a lawyer at forty years of age, but that is not the reason his story is so compelling.

As a boy, in 1952, Paul had contracted polio. He spent nearly all of his time in an iron lung because, without it, he could not survive. Iron lungs are horizontal cylinders that confine their patients. Inhabitants lay inside with only their head protruding from the device. It assisted the individuals breathing, but restricted their movement. Some might be content to stay in the iron lung for security, but not Paul.

He worked relentlessly to teach himself how to forcibly breathe, which enabled him to spend some time outside of the confining device. As a quadriplegic, he found himself forced to hold a rubber-tipped stick in his mouth to turn the pages of his textbooks. While it took him longer to complete his education, he would not be deterred from his goal.

By determination and persistence, Paul completed his law studies in three years, which is the same schedule as other students. He had ample opportunities to use his disability as an excuse for quitting his quest. It would have been easier to blame someone or something else for his condition, but he didn't. Many would expect others or the government to take total care of them, but Paul would not accept those choices.

Paul Alexander inspires me. His is an example that should serve as a role model for us instead of others who achieve less substantive achievement with more opportunity and talent.

He attests that, "The most important thing is faith in self and faith in God. Anything you can dream will come true."[1] How well said!

In spite of persisting when we face adversity, we will not always succeed. I have experienced failures and losses, like most of us will during our lives, and the loss of my son devastated me more than any other. Again, the failure or loss, itself, isn't as important as how we respond to it. It is discouraging, and sometimes embarrassing, to fail, but it would be much worse to quit. As Churchill stirred the British people during World War II, "Never quit, never quit, never quit, never quit, never, never, never, never quit!"

How many great people failed one or more times before they became "overnight" successes? Names such as Abraham Lincoln and Colonel Sanders are but two of an untold number that come to mind. Colonel Sanders, founder of Kentucky Fried Chicken or KFC, began his chicken empire after his 65th birthday.

Abraham Lincoln's path to the presidency is even more inspiring. He failed in business at 22; lost an election for the legislature at 23; failed again in business at 24; won election to the legislature at 25; suffered a nervous breakdown at 27; lost in a race for Speaker at 29; lost an election for Elector at 31; endured defeat in a race for Congress at 34; won election to Congress at 37; lost another race for Congress at 39; lost a race for the Senate at 46; lost running for Vice-President at 47; lost again in a race for the Senate at 49; and finally, found victory when elected President of the United States at 51 years of age. In addition, he won a hotly contested, four-way race for re-election in 1864.

His perseverance and success in overcoming failure and adversity should be an example to us in our quest to achieve our goals. Motivational speaker, T. "Bubba" Bechtol, expresses it like this: "The secret of success in life is not how many times you get knocked down, but how many times you get back up." Abraham Lincoln may be the definitive example of that expression.

Life is full of ups and downs that we must face. The attitude and perspective, though, in which we approach them, and the way we respond to the circumstances we encounter, will result in the experience we gain that prepares us to live our lives to the fullest. Each one of us has the opportunity to affect the results, which lead to our future opportunities.

Principle Twelve

A JOB WELL DONE WILL BE REWARDED

Life is filled with surprises and everyone likes a happy surprise. Thus, as I diligently labored to be the best paperboy that I could be, I didn't expect to receive my first reward and happy surprise of my work life. The autumn in Chicago swiftly evaporated and winter came quicker than my body would accept. In spite of the precipitation, diminishing daylight, and bone chilling cold, the responsibility for delivering my papers remained. As each day moved toward Christmas, I focused more and more on Christmas and the two-week break from school. A few days before Christmas, I received my first happy surprise. While collecting the weekly subscription fee from a customer, she gave me an envelope with additional money as a Christmas bonus. It stunned me, because I had never expected something like this to occur. As I continued my collections, several more customers gave me bonus money. Unaccustomed to this experience, I never developed an expectation to receive a bonus, and thus, I received every bonus with gratitude.

As I reflect on that experience, I realize that the valuable lessons I learned which have positively impacted me since then and permitted me to contribute to society are more important than the cash I received. I learned early on that it didn't matter what company I worked for, if I did my best, I would receive benefits far beyond my compensation. An unknown author stated, "The biggest mistake you can make is to believe that you are working for someone else."

Today, as I mentioned in the introduction, I receive a thinly veiled solicitation for a bonus every year in my newspaper. The attitude is different, the expectation is different, and the appreciation of any bonus is different than the wonderful experience had been privileged to learn so early in my work career.

In every task I attempted during my childhood, my parents and grandparents always stressed the benefit of doing every job to the very best of my abilities. As a child, I didn't understand the importance of the principles that they stressed repeatedly. Fortunately for me, I trusted their teaching and ultimately experienced, from my efforts, why my family proved correct.

Some people believe that you should work at a "get by" pace and they live to pull any energetic soul back to the median level of performance. I disagree wholeheartedly. The moment you succumb to this argument, you have sentenced yourself to mediocrity until you decide to unshackle yourself. **If you want to "get ahead," you have to always do your very best in everything you attempt.**

It doesn't matter if you are throwing papers, shoveling sludge, or digging ditches. Every person's work is valuable and presents an opportunity to strive for excellence. I don't know who said this, but it is true that, "We are what we repeatedly do. Excellence then is not an act, but a habit." When we have excellence as our goal in our every effort, we will achieve more.

You and I alone are responsible for our attitudes and efforts. If we continually work to excel, we will be on an ever-rising path of performance, personal growth, and touching others to enhance lives beyond our vision and life.

The path toward excellence is filled with challenges, demands and uncertainty. It is not for the timid or faint hearted, but for those who are willing to consistently extend themselves and produce excellence. They will discover opportunities, receive rewards and discover real blessings beyond their imagination.

By 1942, Jimmy Doolittle had accomplished many achievements. He had a doctorate in aeronautical sciences. He had proven himself an extremely successful pilot who won many air races and contributed to the growth of aviation. He served in the Army Reserves and had been activated for World War II.

After the attack on Pearl Harbor, December 7th, 1941, Doolittle received orders to lead the first air raid on Japan. The plan devised would be daring from the beginning to its conclusion. For the first time, land-based B-25 bombers would attempt to take off from a moving aircraft carrier.

Upon the completion of their mission, they would fly to occupied China and hopefully land at selected friendly airfields. Like most plans, circumstances would necessitate on-the-fly modifications. In fact, the plan required adaptation from the very beginning.

A day early, and nearly 200 miles before their planned launch, Doolittle and the other 79 men had to take off prematurely. The element of surprise vanished because a Japanese fishing craft had spotted their carrier. In addition, rain and high winds created 30-foot wave crests, making their takeoff even more risky.

No one knew if the bombers could successfully take-off from the carrier because they had been precluded from practicing the actual maneuver. Doolittle chose to go first to demonstrate to the other crews that it could be done. A sigh of relief and increased confidence encompassed everyone as Doolittle's plane successfully lifted off of the flight deck. One by one, the other planes left the deck until all sixteen had taken off of the deck of The Hornet.

Because of the premature departure, every plane would be on its own. The predetermined landing sites could not be reached because the planes would have insufficient fuel to reach them. The probability of return had now been reduced to just above a suicide mission.

The Doolittle raid of April 18, 1942 gave the United States a significant psychological lift at a time of its greatest need. In the aftermath, some planes ditched along the Chinese coast and others crash landed inland. Some of the crewmembers were captured, and three were executed. Fortunately, the Chinese discovered the majority of the crewmembers and provided valuable assistance to facilitate their safe return.

Jimmy Doolittle became an overnight American hero. The Army promoted him from Lt. Colonel to Brigadier General. His two-rank advancement is extremely rare in the military. President Roosevelt personally presented the Congressional Medal of Honor to him.

After his life-defining event, Doolittle received numerous prestigious honors, important military commands, advised U.S. presidents, and achieved business successes.

Doolittle performed many great services for his country. He reaped recognition and rewards for a job well done.

You have the opportunity daily to choose your path. If you are on the path of excellence and doing a job well, congratulations and best wishes for your continued success! If you haven't been on the path of producing excellence, today is the opportunity to change your course. You can do it!

If you are bold and make the move, do not lose heart when you find obstacles in your path. That is the time to bear down. If you don't receive the fruit of your labor immediately, do not become discouraged, but stay the course. If you can't see a reward for all of your hard work, don't quit but be confident that your efforts will not be in vain. If you dedicate yourself to being excellent in your chosen work, you will be rewarded in some way, at some point in time, beyond your wildest dreams.

If you cease your efforts toward excellence, you are not only cheating yourself out of the rewards in store for you, but your family also. In addition, those who you would touch with your efforts would miss out as well. Yes, your life has the potential to impact and change the world in which you live, and your efforts will go a long way in determining your legacy.

A large part of your reputation will be based on your performance at different types of activities, including your work. You have the opportunity to dramatically affect how others perceive you.

How do you want to be perceived in this area? You are the only one who can make this choice. What path will you choose?

Principle Thirteen

THE ESSENTIALNESS OF GOD'S GOOD WILL

Uh oh. Moments before, I felt confident that I could complete my deliveries. Now I wondered, how can I escape the cold instead of finishing my deliveries? I felt worse as I continued. About halfway through my route, as I reached the farthest point away from my house, I came to realize that I couldn't go on. The weather continued to deteriorate, and it grew colder, darker and the visibility lessened because of the falling snow. I desperately began to look for a shelter to protect me from the elements.

This particular day, the high temperature registered at −14 degrees Fahrenheit and the wind howled. Back then, I didn't know about wind-chill factor, but I had never experienced more brutal cold. My mother decided to drive me to deliver my papers, but we could not open the door to the car because it had frozen shut. She implored me to wait until my father came home from work so that he could take me to deliver the papers, but I wouldn't listen. I felt a duty to my customers to deliver the papers in the time frame that met their expectations.

So I left the house that dark and frigid day with my papers and my red "Radio Flyer" wagon in an effort to make my deliveries. Deep snow on the sidewalks made any movement difficult. In addition, the clothing I wore did not protect me sufficiently for the weather that day.

Before long, I felt miserable with cold and shivered, but I kept on. I thought, if I just "toughed it out" that everything would be ok and I could complete my deliveries. Time seemed to move slowly and each paper I delivered seemed to take longer and longer. Eventually, finding shelter became more important than completing my route.

Fortunately, I found a gas station open and the employees welcomed me inside. I didn't realize how cold I had become until I stood below the heater inside the station. The station manager permitted me to borrow his phone and I called my parents. They expressed worry about my safety and responded with joy to hear that I had found a place of refuge. My mother told me to stay put until my father could come and pick me up.

My body warmed slowly as I awaited the arrival of my father, which seemed to take longer than I'm sure it actually did. He and my brother arrived to pluck me from my haven and the three of us left. They dropped me off at the house and my parents and brother delivered the remainder of the papers.

Back at home, after they completed delivering the papers, my mother worked diligently to overcome the effects of the cold. While I didn't suffer frostbite, to this day my toes and several fingers are extremely sensitive to the least amount of cold. They easily become painful at the first sign of the temperature dropping and serve as a reminder of my ignorance and how the situation could have resulted in tragedy.

This is probably the most difficult characteristic to discuss, because of the variety of opinions people have and the reactions that result from its discussion. I believe that the God of the Bible exists, is in control of the universe, and touches my life daily. I have failed him many times, but HE has never failed me. No, there are many more times than I can share in this volume that HIS benevolence has spared, provided for or forgiven me.

In retrospect, God spared me injury or worse. I don't know why. I didn't recognize it at the time, but looking back it is obvious to me. When I look back over my life, I see many other examples where I experienced protection. In high school, when I delivered prescriptions for a pharmacy, I came storming back into the store moments after an armed robber left. A small difference in timing could have dramatically changed the outcome. I have had several other close calls that I am thankful turned out the way they did instead of in a much worse manner.

I believe that God has been personally involved in the details of my life. HE has intervened many times for purposes that haven't totally been revealed. When I review the successes and failures I have experienced, I see a stark contrast. In every setback, I see my own decisions and individual effort, which resulted in the negative result. In each and every experience, where I have achieved a positive result, I see HIS loving touch, direction and good will without which I would not have achieved the success. If I follow HIM, I will succeed. If I rely on myself, I will fall short and miss out on the blessings HE has in store for me.

The road to his success had been long and paved with obstacles. Extended separation from his family, several relocations, and working hard in a very competitive environment served as some of the prerequisites to attain his goal.

By the mid-1980's, Dave Dravecky had it all. He had a beautiful wife and family. He lived his dream as a starting pitcher with the San Francisco Giants.

Just as he realized his greatest career success, doctors discovered cancer in his pitching arm. After surgery and follow-up treatments, Dravecky underwent a long and arduous rehabilitation. Finally, he pitched again in the major leagues.

Poised to return to the level of his previous performance, Dave then suffered another setback. As he threw a pitch in a game, a loud pop sounded and Dravecky fell to the ground in excruciating pain.

In addition to the broken arm, cancer had reappeared. Doctors found themselves compelled to amputate the arm that

Dravecky had used to achieve success and earn a living. His life-long dream had been derailed. How would he respond?

Through it all, Dave Dravecky spoke of his faith enabling him to cope and endure every misfortune. Instead of focusing on the negative, he focused on the positive. He realized that life is lived day by day. He knew God loved him and would help him face every challenge that would arise in his in life.

Today, Dave is a public speaker, author, and President of Outreach of Hope Ministries. He speaks on his faith, providing encouragement and hope to others on how to face the daily challenges in life and suffering. He has, and continues to, inspire many. His example shows the importance of attempting to make something positive out of every hardship.

The scripture he lives by gave Laura and me peace and hope when we lost our son, John. 2nd Corinthians 4:16-18 states, "Therefore we do not lose heart. Though outwardly we are wasting away, yet inwardly we are being renewed day by day. For our light and momentary troubles are achieving for us an eternal glory that far outweighs them all. So we fix our eyes not on what is seen, but what is unseen. For what is seen is temporary, but what is unseen is eternal."

We each have a choice in our lives of going it alone, asking the help of others, and/or seeking the help of the ONE who is able to provide for our every need. It took me some time to realize the difference in that choice and others, and I most certainly missed out on some benefits because of my decisions. My hope for you is that you don't delay in recognizing what is there for you, and that you, and everyone you touch, are positively impacted because of your decisions.

Principle Fourteen

YOUR THRESHOLD, YOUR FUTURE, YOUR CHOICE

"Today is the first day of the rest of your life" is a cliché that burst onto the scene years ago. It is powerful. People used it, overused it, and abused it. People finally discarded it. But, trite as it is, it is true.

As you look at the cover of this volume, you will notice images that you see everyday, but you may not actively notice. As you open the door of your home, you prepare to venture from an area of comfort and security into the world. We are given the gift of life one day at a time.

Each day, we have an opportunity to achieve our dreams and goals. While we may not achieve an objective on any given day, we can always take steps toward achieving a desired result. At the end of the day, can we say that we made progress or will we discover that we squandered our time that day? "Carpe diem!" Seize the day! The open door reflects the new day of opportunity. How will you use it? It is your choice.

There are three things that will affect your experience each day. The first is your **attitude** as you cross the threshold and enter the world. As we discussed in Chapter Two, I firmly believe that a positive outlook is most beneficial to us in everything we experience. Consciously or not, we choose, each day, the attitude we will have as we face the world. The time of day or weather should not adversely impact our attitude as we walk through the doorway. The threshold represents our portal. The sun may or may not shine. It doesn't matter. What does matter is how we view what circumstances we encounter. How do you view the world as you enter it each day? It is your choice.

The second thing that will impact our response to circumstances is our **perspective of life**. Volumes have, and can be, written about this subject alone. For purposes of the volume of this book, we will limit our discussion. Questions for our consideration are many. Do we make decisions based solely on the situation of the moment? Do we have a religious faith that directs our views of daily events? Do we think of the affects of our decision for the present only? Do we think of the influence of our decision for the remainder of our life? Do we think of the consequences of our decision on our family, friends and those we care about? Do we think about the affects of our decision on those we don't know, but may be impacted by our decision? Heavy, I know, but important.

The world pushes us to consider the moment and ourselves only. If we're not careful, it is easy to make decisions based solely on those parameters that we will regret later. What basis will you make your decisions on? The choice is yours.

The final thing that can affect our experience each day is the news or actions of others that you encounter. It may come in the form of a newspaper, by radio or television, word of mouth, or any other personal experience. What happens is not as important as **how you respond to daily events**.

On September 11, 2001, the defining event of our time occurred. Each of us had to respond to our own circumstances, but President Bush, Governor Pataki of New York State, Mayor Giuliani of New York City and others had responsibilities to their citizens as well. Not only did what they do in response to the attacks make an impact, but also their attitude and approach proved instrumental in comforting and encouraging millions of people to face the uncertainty that terrorists ushered into the world that day.

Our world changed for the foreseeable future on September 11th. There have been, and will continue to be, many ups and downs since that day. Do we let each individual piece of news affect our outlook on life? Are we unaware of what is going on, to the point of missing opportunities that could benefit our life? How will we respond to the events of the day? The choice is yours.

Life is full of choices and our life experience will reflect the sum of our choices. We will all look back on choices that we are glad we made and some decisions where we can admit we made mistakes. An expression in which we can aspire says, "If you're going to make a mistake, make sure each one is a new one." I wish I could claim that every mistake I have made, and make, is a new one, but I can't. We can strive to learn from our mistakes in the effort to minimize the times we repeat a mistake. Still, you and I can constantly work to improve our choices in order to realize our dreams. In our efforts, we may uncover unforeseen gifts.

Bill crossed his threshold daily for more than forty years and went into the world as a door-to-door salesman of products for the home. Each day he walked 7–10 miles in the Portland, Oregon area, regardless of the weather or circumstances. The work was hard, the pain constant and rejection was common, but Bill pressed on to do his duty without complaint. He still sells everyday, although he has been forced by age and physical limitations to give up his door-to-door routine.

Bill is no common individual, but his accomplishments of ordinary tasks are extraordinary. For you see, Bill Porter was born with cerebral palsy. His disease limits his ability to speak, to walk, and makes it difficult for him to write. In addition, it affected his appearance on the doorstep of prospects enough to make some people feel uncomfortable in his presence.

Early on, his mother and father taught him that he would have to learn how to provide for himself. In spite of the availability of government assistance programs, Bill's parents declined to take advantage of them. They knew that the only sure way to make certain he was taken care of after their passing was to teach him to be self sufficient.

With his mother's encouragement after his father's death, he decided that he would like to be a salesman. His efforts at finding employment were extremely discouraging, but after a persistent effort, he persuaded The Watkins Company to give him a chance to work as a door-to-door salesman on straight commission.

At first, his mother assisted him and later he hired a personal assistant to help him do the little things that most of us take for granted. He required help tying his shoes and tie and buttoning his shirts. He needed assistance in typing and delivering his orders. Still, he didn't use these challenges as excuses for not working and succeeding.

Bill overcame his initial butterflies enough to begin knocking on doors. For too long, he was ignored, rejected and told by his prospects that they were not interested in his products. But, he persisted! Eventually, people began opening their homes to allow him to show his wares. When someone decided to make a purchase, they had to write their own order form because of Bill's physical limitations. Upon leaving a house, an observer couldn't tell if Bill made a sale or not because his demeanor was constant. He knew right from the start that selling is a numbers game and that success is predicated on the quality and quantity of effort he exerted regardless of the responses he received.

Eventually Bill rose to the rank of top retail salesman for Watkins. He was the last door-to-door salesman for the company. Now at seventy-two, he has discontinued selling door-to-door, but continues to sell to long time customers and via the Internet.

Bill Porter is the epitome of someone who has a positive attitude, approaches everything with a long-term perspective and has positively responded to the challenges of his life in an example worthy of everyone's emulation.

When I hear my sales reps complain about their quota, territory, competition or give other reasons they can't succeed, I think of Bill Porter. When I have a negative thought about my business, I think of Bill Porter. When I think of Bill Porter, I think about how great the United States of America is to give us the freedom to be whatever we can, and the opportunity to try any work we desire. I think of how wonderful it is to be able to be paid as much as we're worth, and to have the opportunity to move up from any economic class of citizen to another class based on our individual effort.

Bill Porter inspires us to attempt to be more than we believe we can be. His example of an indefatigable desire to succeed reminds us that the largest obstacles to our success are the limitations that we place on ourselves.

Today, we stand on the threshold of unlimited opportunity. The world beckons and we must choose whether we will leave this world without changing it or whether we will make a difference. What we do in the **present** will create a **past** that greatly influences our opportunities and dreams in the **future**.

Our lifetime of choices will create our legacy.

Our final question is what can I do today to improve life for my family, my community and myself? The choice is yours and mine.

Afterword

What life lessons can you learn from a seemingly simple job held at a young age?

Using the analogy of a paperboy's "career," Battle has gleaned life-long value from routine daily events. As a former paperboy, I can attest to the issues of dealing with extreme weather, the extra heavy Thursday papers and the customers who would not be "at home" when they knew you were coming to collect their payments. Each of these situations was not recognized as an educational event at the time. However, I have found, as did Battle, that they paid dividends in my character development.

Battle has also increased the validity of these individual lessons by linking them to situations faced by world leaders in decisions that built and demonstrated their character.

This is a very timely book. Today, media screams out to young people to look out for themselves. Instant gratification is critical. This book reminds them that true character and satisfaction only comes from personal achievements that start small but can become cumulatively important.

The old fashioned (maybe the new fashioned) idea that you can find benefits far beyond immediate gratification by performing serious and consistent work is refreshing. This work can have multiple results. First, you have the personal satisfaction of doing something well. Secondly, you compile a personal track record of achievement. Last and maybe most importantly, it pays unrecognized (at the time) long-term benefits.

Most of us have experienced the excitement of a part-time or summer job only to become bored after several weeks in the position. Battle has taken the time to reflect on the long-term learning that resulted from his particular experience. He raises the issue as to whether there are similar experiences in our life that can or will lead to our valuable life-long learning.

William White
Retired Chairman / C.E.O,
Bell & Howell Company
Professor, Northwestern University

Appendix A

QUOTATIONS

Be Responsible

Dedication: The ability and determination to complete a resolution long after the mood in which it was made is gone.
— Unknown

Sometimes it is not enough to do your best. Sometimes you have to do what is required.
— Winston Churchill

Success is 90% showing up.
— Woody Allen

You can't build a reputation on what you're going to do.
— Henry Ford

You Will Achieve More With a Positive Attitude Than With a Negative One

If you think you're too big for a small job, then you are too small for a big job.

— Unknown

Whether you think you can, or think you can't, you're right.

— Henry Ford

Can't never did anything.

— Bill Battle

It is amazing what one can accomplish when one doesn't know what one can't do.

— Unknown

Things turn out best for the people who make the best of the way things turn out.

— Basketball coach John Wooden

Have Confidence

It is the saddest of all mistakes to do nothing when you can only do a little. Do what you can.

— Sydney Smith

Challenges that are bigger than men make men bigger.

— Unknown

A winner never stops trying.
— Dallas Cowboys coach Tom Landry

To achieve all that is possible, we must attempt the impossible. To be as much as we can be, we must dream of being more.
— Fred LaNovel

It is not the critic who counts, not the man who points out how the strong man stumbled or where the doer of deeds could have done better. The credit belongs to the man who is actually in the arena; whose face is marred by dust and sweat and blood; who strives valiantly; who errs and comes short again and again; who knows the great enthusiasms; the great devotions, and spends himself in a worthy cause; who, at best, knows in the end the triumph of high achievement; and who; at the worst, if he fails, at least fails while daring greatly, so his place shall NEVER be with those cold and timid souls who know neither victory nor defeat.
— Theodore Roosevelt

The Value of Money

The man who overestimates the value of money will never be happy by amassing more of it.
— Unknown

The value of money lies altogether in the uses to which it is put.
— Unknown

Of all the valuable things that money can't buy, the most valuable is the man who can't be bought.

— Unknown

For the love of money is a root of all kinds of evil.

— 1st Timothy 6:10

The Benefit of Differed Gratification

The dictionary is the only place in the world where success comes before work.

— Unknown

A sluggard does not plow in season; so at harvest time he looks but finds nothing.

— Proverbs 20:4

Admit Your Mistakes and People Will Usually Forgive You

If you're going to make a mistake, make sure each one is a new one.

— Unknown

The Quality of Your Service Matters

When you're good to others, you're best to yourself.

— Benjamin Franklin

The mortal enemy of best is good.

— H. E. Butt

Not doing more than the average is what keeps the average down.

— Unknown

Patience Must Be Learned

Have patience with all things, but first with yourself. Never confuse your mistakes with your value as a human being. You're a perfectly valuable, creative, worthwhile person simply because you exist. And no amount of triumphs or tribulations can ever change that. Unconditional self-acceptance is the core of a peaceful mind.

— St. Francis de Sales

A patient man has great understanding, but a quick-tempered man displays folly.

— Proverbs 14:29

There is Synergy in Teamwork

It is one of the most beautiful compensations of this life that no man can sincerely try to help another without helping himself.

— Emerson

The Best Leadership is By Example

How can I hear what you say, when what you do speaks so loudly?

— Unknown

Do not follow where the path may lead. Go instead where there is no path and leave a trail.

— Unknown

Leadership is the ability to get people to do what they don't want to do, but what they need to do to become better.

— Tom Landry

Be sure you're right, then go ahead.

— Davy Crockett

Persist in The Face of Adversity

In life, you'll have your back against the wall many times. You might as well get used to it.

— Football coach Paul "Bear" Bryant

The secret of success in life is not how many times you get knocked down, but how many times you get back up.

— Bubba Bechtol

Obstacles are those frightful things you see when you take your eyes off the goal.

— Unknown

Adversity reveals genius and prosperity conceals it.

— Horace

It's always too soon to quit.

— Lewis R. Timberlake

Never quit; never quit; never quit; never quit; never, never, never, never, quit!

— Winston Churchill

A Job Well Done Will Be Rewarded

People forget how fast you did a job, but they remember how well you did it.

— Unknown

Well done is better than well said.

— Benjamin Franklin

We are what we repeatedly do. Excellence then is not an act, but a habit.

— Unknown

The biggest mistake you can make is to believe that you are working for someone else.

— Unknown

Every job is a self-portrait of the person who did it. Autograph your work with excellence.

— Unknown

It is not the honor that you take with you, but the heritage you leave behind.
— Baseball manager and general manager Branch Rickey

The Essentialness of God's Good Will

And God is able to make all grace abound to you, so that in all things at all times, having all that you need, you will abound in every good work.
— 2 Corinthians 9:7-8

Other Beneficial Quotations

Don't pray for tasks equal to your strengths. Pray for strength equal to your tasks.
— President George W. Bush

What you are is God's gift to you. What you become is your gift to God.
— Sam Chase

Destiny is not a matter of chance; it is a matter of choice.
— William Jennings Bryan

The price of excellence is discipline. The price of mediocrity is disappointment.
— William A. Ward

Don't get engrossed over the things you have no control or it will adversely affect the things you can control.

— John Wooden

Whatever you do, work at it with all your heart, as working for the Lord, not for men.

— Colossian 3:23

Appendix B

A - Z Characteristics of a Good Work Ethic

A — Arrive on time!

B — The boss is the boss.

C — Courage / Confidence / Creativity / Coachable

D — Deferred Gratification

E — Enthusiasm

F — Flexibility

G — Goal Oriented

H — High Energy

I — Initiative

J — Join Together — Teamwork!

K — Keep On — Persistence!

L — Lead by Example

M — Money Motivated

N — Negotiation Skills

O — Organized

P — Positive Attitude / Poised / Patience

Q — Quick on Your Feet

R — Responsible

S — Show up Every Day

T — Trustworthy

U — Undeniable (Oral) Communication Skills

V — Value of Money

W — Watchful (Observant)

X — Complete The Job! (X or Sign off)

Y — Why? Why Not? / Good Questioner

Z — Zealous

Appendix C

BATTLE'S BULLETS

- What you do in the **present** will create a **past** that will greatly influence your opportunities and dreams in the **future**.

- Easy way out is an oxymoron.

- Work is the four-letter word that builds character

- Things can always be worse.

- Things are never as bad as they may appear to be at the moment.

- The earlier you face rejection, and learn how to respond to it, the better you will be prepared for it when it comes in the future.

- People value honesty over anything else in a relationship.

- Everything you do today will impact your future.

- Like many other characteristics essential to our success and happiness, patience is one that we are not born with, but hopefully will learn through the rigors of experience.

- It doesn't matter how old you are, or what position you hold in society. You influence others by your actions, whether they are positive or negative.

- The true test of a man's character is how he responds to adversity.

- If you want to "get ahead," you have to always do your very best in everything you attempt.

- Striving for consensus is not leadership.

Appendix D

Recommended Reading

1. *Born to Win*, by Lewis Timberlake

2. *The Right Moment*, by William Hyche.

3. *The Language of Conscience*, by Tieman H. Dippel, Jr.

NOTES

Principle 2 —
You Will Achieve More with a Positive Attitude than a Negative One

1. D'Souza, Dinesh. *Ronald Reagan: How an Ordinary Man Became an Extraordinary Leader.* New York: The Free Press, 1997. 253.

Principle 3 —
Have Confidence

1. Trulock, Alice Rains. *In The Hands Of Providence.* Chapel Hill: The University of North Carolina Press, 1992. 154-155.

Principle 4 —
The Value of Money

1. Walton, Sam. *Made In America.* New York: Doubleday, 1992. 5.

2. Ibid. 10.

Principle 5 —
The Benefit of Deferred Gratification

1. Brokaw, Tom. *The Greatest Generation.* New York: Random House, 1998, xx.

Principle 8 —
Patience Must Be Learned

1. Cannadine, David- Editor. *Blood, Sweat and Tears.* Boston: Houghton, Mifflin Co., 1989, 178.

Principle 11 —
Persist in the Face of Adversity

1. Frink, Cheryl Coggins. *Keeping Faith.* Austin: Austin American Statesman, 1986, A8.

Bibliography

Battle, Richard. *Surviving Grief by God's Grace.* Bloomington, Indiana: 1stBooks Library, 2002.

Battle, Richard. *The Volunteer Handbook: How to Organize and Manage a Successful Organization.* Austin, Texas: Volunteer Concepts, 1988.

Beard, Ross. *Carbine.* Williamstown, New Jersey: Phillips Publications, 1977.

Bohle, Bruce. *The Home Book of American Quotations.* New York, New York: Dodd, Mead & Company, 1967.

Brokaw, Tom. *The Greatest Generation.* New York: Random House, 1998.

Cbsportline.com

Covey, Stephen R. *The 7 Habits of Highly Effective People.* New York, New York: Fireside, 1989.

Doolittle, James H. *I Could Never Be So Lucky Again.* New York: Bantam, 1991.

Dravecky, Dave. *Comeback.* Grand Rapids: Zondervan, 1990.

D'Souza, Dinesh. *Ronald Reagan: How an Ordinary Man Became an Extraordinary Leader.* New York: The Free Press, 1997.

Frink, Cheryl Coggins. *Keeping Faith.* Austin: Austin American Statesman, 1986.

Hallman, Tom Jr. *Life of a salesman.* Portland: The Oregonian, 1995.

Loverro, Thom. *The Quotable Coach: Leadership and Motivation From History's Greatest Coaches.* Franklin Lakes, New Jersey: Career Press, 2002.

Manchester, William. *The Last Lion: Alone, 1932-1940.* Boston: Little, Brown, 1988.

McPherson, James M. *Battle Cry of Freedom.* Oxford: Oxford University Press, 1988.

Moore, Stephen. *Eighteen Minutes.* Lanham, Republic of Texas Press, 2004.

Phillips, Donald. *Lincoln on Leadership.* New York: Warner Books, 1992.

Powers, Kay. *Circus Veteran Ambitious at age 102.* Austin: Austin American Statesman, 1986.

Timberlake, Lewis R. *It's Always Too Soon To Quit.* Grand Rapids: Revell, 1988.

Trulock, Alice Rains. *In the Hands of Providence.* Chapel Hill: The University of North Carolina Press, 1992.

Walton, Sam. *Made In America.* New York: Doubleday, 1992.

Ziglar, Zig. *Secrets of Closing The Sale.* Old Tappan, New Jersey: Fleming H. Revell, 1982.

Index

A
Alexander, Paul 94, 95
Allen, Woody 119
Alone 74

B
B-25 Bomber 100
Battle, Bill 120
Battle, Elizabeth 28, 49, 59
Battle, Jerry 77
Battle, John 29, 107
Battle, Laura 50, 107
Bechtol, T. Bubba 96, 124
Berlin Wall 33
Birmingham, England 66
Bowdoin College 38
Brokaw, Tom 52, 135, 137
Bryan, William Jennings 126
Bryant, Paul "Bear" 124
Buoniconti, Nick 79
Bush, George W., President 111, 126
Butt, H. E. 69, 123

C
Carbine Williams, Movie 59
Cbsportline.com 79, 137
Chamberlain, Joshua 38, 39
Chase, Sam 126
Chicago American, newspaper 20, 23, 35
China 100
Churchill, Sir Winston 74, 75, 95, 119, 125
Cold War 33
Covey, Stephen 80, 137
Crockett, David (Davy) 88, 124

D
Dallas Cowboys 79, 86, 121
Doolittle, James H. 99, 100, 101, 137
Dravecky, Dave 106, 107, 137

E
Emerson, Ralph Waldo 82, 123

F
Ford, Henry 28, 119, 120
Franklin, Benjamin 70, 122, 125

G
Gettysburg, Movie 38
Giuliani, Rudolph 111

H
Houston, Sam 86
Huchingson, C.B. 57

J

Junior Chamber of Commerce (Jaycees) 80

K

Kennedy, John, President 80
Kentucky Fried Chicken (KFC) 95

L

Landry, Tom 79, 86, 121, 124
LaNovel, Fred 121
Lincoln, Abraham, President 25, 26, 95, 96, 138
Little Round Top 39
London, England 67

M

M-1 Carbine 61
Manchester, William 74, 138
Miami Dolphins 78, 79
Muscular Dystrophy Association (MDA) 80, 81

N

NFL (National Football League) 78
NFL Hall of Fame 79
No-Name Defense 79

O

Outreach of Hope Ministries 107

P

Pataki, George 111
Porter, Bill 112, 113, 114
Prohibition 59

R

Radio Flyer 104
Reagan, Ronald, President 32, 33, 34, 135, 137

Reykjavik, Iceland 33
Rickey, Branch 126
Roosevelt, Franklin, President 101
Roosevelt, Theordore, President 121

S

St. Francis de Sales 123
San Francisco Giants 106
Sanders, Col. (Harlan) 95
Soviet Union 33
Super Bowl (VI, VII, VIII) 78, 79
Surviving Grief by Gods Grace 29, 137, 141

T

Texas Army 87
The Seven Habits of Highly Successful People 80
Timberlake, Lewis 125
20th Maine 39

U

USS Hornet 100

W

Wal-Mart 45, 46
Walton, Sam 45, 46, 135, 138
Ward, William 126
Watkins Co. 113
Williams, David Marshall (Carbine) 59, 60, 61
Winchester Co. 61
Wooden, John 120, 127
World War II 51, 59, 61, 74, 75, 95, 99

Z

Ziglar, Zig 82, 138

About The Author

Richard Battle has 32 years experience in sales, management and leadership in various business entities. He was selected to the National Register's Who's Who in Executives and Professionals in 2005.

Richard has previously authored, *The Volunteer Handbook — How to Organize and Manage a Successful Organization.* He has served on the board and in leadership roles in many organizations including The John Ben Shepperd Public Leadership Foundation, Boy Scouts of America, Muscular Dystrophy Association and Keep Austin Beautiful.

As president of the Austin Junior Chamber of Commerce (83-84), the U.S. Junior Chamber of Commerce recognized the chapter as the Most Outstanding chapter in the United States, and Junior Chamber of Commerce International recognized Richard as the Outstanding Chapter President in the world.

He also authored, *"Surviving Grief by God's Grace."*
Richard has been a public speaker and trainer for over

twenty years on topics including voluntarism, leadership and motivation.

Richard, his wife Laura, and daughter Elizabeth live in Austin, Texas.

For additional information on scheduling
speaking engagements, or seminars,
or to write to Richard Battle.

Please address your correspondence to:

Richard Battle
P. O. Box 341911
Austin, Texas 78734

www.richardbattle.com

or call
1-888-WKETHIC (953-8442)